FAMILY AND WORK

Economic Policy Council of the UNA–USA

FAMILY AND WORK
Bridging the Gap

edited by
SYLVIA ANN HEWLETT
ALICE S. ILCHMAN
JOHN J. SWEENEY

BALLINGER PUBLISHING COMPANY
Cambridge, Massachusetts
A Subsidiary of Harper & Row, Publishers, Inc.

International Standard Book Number: 0-88730-066-9

Library of Congress Catalog Card Number: 86-20571

Printed in the United States of America

Library of Congress Cataloging-in-Publication Data

Family and work.

   Based on rewritten and edited versions of papers commissioned by the UNA-USA Economic Policy Council.
   Bibliography: p.
   Includes index.
   1. Work and family—United States.   I. Hewlett, Sylvia Ann.
II. Ilchman, Alice Stone.   III. Sweeney, John J., 1934-
IV. United Nations Association of the United States of America.
Economic Policy Council.
HD4904.25.F37   1986   306.8'7   86-20571
ISBN 0-88730-066-9

The United Nations Association of the USA (UNA–USA) is a private, nonprofit organization which conducts programs of research, study and information to broaden public understanding of the activities of the United Nations and other multilateral institutions. Through its nationwide membership and network of affiliated national organizations, UNA–USA informs and involves the public in foreign affairs issues, and encourages constructive U.S. policies on global issues.

The UNA-USA Economic Policy Council is comprised of a cross-section of U.S. business, labor and academic leaders who are brought together in study panels to analyze important international issues affecting long-run U.S. relationships with both developed and developing countries. The EPC both identifies critical policy questions and makes recommendations which are then published and presented to Congress, the Administration, international organizations, and the U.S. private sector. As part of this process, a number of papers are commissioned from leading specialists.

This UNA-USA Economic Policy Council Book is based on rewritten and edited versions of some of these papers. UNA-USA is responsible for the choice of the subject areas and the decision to publish the volumes, but the responsibility for the content of the papers and for opinions expressed in them rests with the individual authors and editors.

This book was made possible by generous grants from The Ford Foundation and The Rockefeller Foundation.

083690

CONTENTS

LIST OF FIGURES AND TABLES

xi

PREFACE

The Economic Policy Council (EPC) of the United Nations Association of the United States chose to undertake this study in order to examine the extent of ongoing changes that are affecting the family, the workplace, and the economy. The tremendous growth in the rate of women's labor force participation, the escalating divorce rate, and the increasing number of single-parent families have all contributed to the transformation of the workplace and the traditional family structure. Working parents are increasingly unsure of how to balance the competing pressures of job and family responsibilities. Yet major institutions in our country—from the federal government to the workplace—have not fully recognized or responded to these changes. Most industrialized countries have implemented family policies to accommodate the changing economic and social environment. The United States has not. A national family policy would strengthen the foundation of the family and the competitiveness of the economy by providing a supportive infrastructure that would enable parents to successfully mediate the competing demands of work and family life and would contribute to worker productivity.

Participants in this project included business executives, labor leaders, economists, and international experts. Some participants contributed papers, and all took part in our panel discussions. The chapters that constitute this volume serve a twofold purpose: They offer a detailed analysis of work and family issues and provide insights into how different actors in the U.S. economy, and foreign observers view these issues.

This project is part of the ongoing attempt of the EPC to orchestrate a systematic and constructive involvement in international economic problems by the U.S. private sector. The EPC is committed to representing the views of both management and labor, who work in close cooperation with economists and other professionals to analyze international economic problems facing the United States and to develop policy recommendations. Because these policy recommendations are grounded in extensive research and discussion, and because they are backed by a broad domestic consensus, they have a special legitimacy for U.S. policymakers. The EPC is one of the most experienced labor and management groups working in the area of international economic policy, and it is our hope that by contributing a thorough analysis of work and family life in the United States and other industrialized countries, this study will help bring about the necessary responses from the various institutions in our society to the dramatic changes that have taken place.

We would like to express our appreciation to The Ford Foundation and The Rockefeller Foundation for providing grants that have helped make this study possible. We would also like to thank Judy Farrell for her sterling efforts in orchestrating this study and Pam Laber for her research and analysis.

The views expressed in these chapters are solely those of the individual authors. The consensus findings and recommendations of the panel members who participated in this study were published in a separate report of the Economic Policy Council of the UNA–USA.

Sylvia Ann Hewlett
Alice S. Ilchman
John J. Sweeney

1 INTRODUCTION

Alice S. Ilchman

The members of the Family Policy Panel of the Economic Policy Council of the United Nations Association of the United States met with considerable difficulty in sitting down to their task. Those several dozen scholars, leaders of corporations, and leaders of labor were committed to their work — that is, developing a policy initiative in support of working parents in the United States. We knew from our own lives, our studies, or our responsibilities in the workplace that workers increasingly find their parental and economic roles in conflict. We knew that families had been profoundly transformed in the last three decades by the entry of women into the labor force and that most children today have a working mother. We were also concerned that the fastest-growing family type was that headed by a single parent and that female-headed households are, more often than not, poor households. Not a few of us were dismayed to discover that children, especially preschoolers, have become the largest disadvantaged age group in the United States. (In 1984 a poor citizen was twice as likely to be a 3-year-old as a 70-year-old; the poverty rate was 24 percent among preschool children, 12 percent among the elderly, and 11 percent among the adult population (U.S. Bureau of the Census 1985).)

Despite that litany of concerns, there were still other reasons our panel members were drawn to this task. The Economic Policy Council panel that preceded ours, John Filer's and Douglas Fraser's panel

1

on *Jobs in the 1980s* found that it was difficult to talk of future jobs without talking specifically of future workers. The jobs panel noted the majority of new workers entering the labor force in the next decade would be women, especially mothers of school-age children, which would exacerbate the growing conflict that parents felt between their work and family responsibilities. That panel urged us to get on with our task.

Some panel members were most concerned about the growing numbers of impoverished children and the negative implications for a future skilled workforce and responsible citizenry. Others were most concerned about stresses on family stability or opportunities for women. All were puzzled by the allocation of U.S. public and private resources that make most parenting leaves and child care support too expensive even when these are intimately connected to productivity in the workplace. And a number of us looked for insights into our dilemma by examining other western democracies that had managed to support high proportions of working parents with extended social support systems.

Why, then, was it difficult to pursue the panel's agenda? In part, it was a question of individual priorities. At some level, men believe that family policy is a women's problem; corporate folk believe it is a labor problem; and older parents believe it is a problem of younger parents or at least those with young children. Consequently, it is hard to get down to business in a tightly scheduled day when the subject is somebody else's problem, when the topic has been regarded in this country as a highly personal concern, and when, in any event, any solution will be complicated and expensive.

Nonetheless, we persevered. Fully aware of the unresponsive economic and social climate into which our report would be sent, we differed on the most effective basic thrust. Some of us believed that the shock value and the shame of the disadvantaged children were most arresting; others believed that the ill-prepared and ill-nourished future labor force, with consequent declines in productivity and wealth, would be more persuasive to those who believe that the United States cannot afford to extend social programs. Other panel members felt that action was most likely to be taken when those holding power also shared the problem and had an immediate interest in its amelioration. (We recalled the prompt attention paid to cuts in the government student aid when the Guaranteed Student Loans to the middle class were threatened along with grants to the poor.) Therefore, it was argued, our committee should emphasize that an employed mother is "everyman's" mother, wife, or daughter. Nearly 70 percent of mothers with school-age children work outside the home, it was argued, and support for these parents is needed as surely as for the single mother in the urban ghetto, although the former will have more resources to put toward her solution. In addition, it is hardly lost on the rising middle-class worker that payments on 65 percent of all new home mortgages, the symbol of the American dream, require two paychecks.

The result of our efforts, *Work and Family in the United States: A Policy Initiative*, was published in December 1985, and its presentation reflected the differences in the views of the panel members. It is a spare volume with succinct recommendations. Much of the subtlety and argument behind the recommendations, and all of the comparative material from other countries, had to be published elsewhere: It is happily contained in this volume, *Family and Work: Bridging the Gap*.

In retrospect, our panel might well have spent more time on three issues. One is the consideration of maternity leaves as uniquely different from all other disabilities. Although throughout history protective legislation for women has in the long run worked against the best interests and greater opportunities of women, treating childbirth as an ordinary "disability" may in fact be the wrong approach. Childbirth is hardly stereotyped behavior that, given more experience, women will overcome, and presumably its outcome has more social good than an appendectomy or recovery from mental depression. It happens relatively few times in a woman's life, and there is a very narrow range for satisfactory "alternative arrangements." Legislation could protect "the worker giving childbirth" rather than "women" and perhaps sidestep some of the unavoidable issues involved in the discussion.

A second area that bears scrutiny is how working parents can be helped with the costs of caring for their children in the preschool years, especially in infancy. What strikes most persons concerned with buying or providing child care in the early years is its extraordinary cost. Perhaps more assistance is due the parent/worker who is willing to subsidize through reduced compensation the high cost of child care. Such a parent, unable to forgo total income through resignation or unpaid leave, would find caring for his or her own child an attractive tradeoff to reduced income. Whether the costs of paying for child care could be assumed publicly through tax credits, or borne by the employer as well as by the worker in reduced wages, is controversial. But it is strikingly inefficient that incentives for reducing the cost of child care for brief periods in early infancy are insufficiently explored.

Perhaps a change in the federal tax code would most facilitate what we are after. A government with a "hands-off" policy on family matters nonetheless makes significant family policy through tax provisions or the absence thereof. The major vehicle of federal government support for child care comes through a child care tax credit that is available to parents as a percentage of qualified child care expenditures up to a maximum of $4,800 for two or more children until age 15. The other benefit that the government extends for child care is the untaxed fringe benefit of employer-provided day care.

Although our panel gave high priority to extending the child care credit, we did not invest our energy in specific models or recommendations to send into the tumultuous environment for tax reform. President Reagan announced in 1985 that tax reform would be a major goal of his second term, and many energetic players already were in the game. Large as the child care tax credit loomed on the horizon of support for children, it was a relatively small part of the proposed tax reforms. In retrospect, we should have riveted our attention on Treasury I, as the proposed reform came to be called, and on the suggested increases for the personal exemption. An early version of the tax reform called for doubling the current exemption of $1,040 to $2,000. Changes in the personal deduction could have far greater effect on families with children than extending the child care tax credit, since a major goal of tax reform was to simplify the deductions and redistribute back to the general population the revenue not thus collected.

Let us see how this might work and its advantages for families with children. In 1948 family incomes became taxable at $2,667, calculated as the $600 personal exemption (times four) plus the $267 standard deduction. The median income for a family of four in the same year was $3,468.[1] This meant that three-quarters of the median family income in 1948 was exempt from federal tax. Whether or not thus intended, the government in those years chose not to tax income that could be calculated as the basic cost of raising a family. By 1983 the median income for a family of four was $29,184, and according to the Joint Committee on Taxation, federal income tax was applied beginning at $8,785: Less than one-third of median family income was exempt.

Over the years we have seen a flattening of the tax pyramid. Marginal rates of 80 percent at the top have been reduced to 50 percent, and taxes at the lower end have increased substantially. Inflation pushed families into higher brackets, and social security tax, which applies to the first dollar earned, grew steadily. The result is a significantly higher tax bite into the income of median (and certainly poor) families than in 1948. The result should startle us.

We would need $5,600 today to maintain the value of the 1948 personal exemption of $600. If we assume that the personal exemption should have some bearing on the costs of raising a child (not at all to be assumed but certainly a rational enough calculation), we would need to know how far the costs per year of raising a child have outstripped the value of the personal exemption. Families now spend per year something like $4,600 per child (Moynihan 1986: 161), and the dependent exemption hovers at $1,040. Why not make the personal exemption equal to the minimal cost of supporting a child? Raising children would be affirmed as valuable to society if the taxable income for a family of four began at $22,400 (personal exemption adjusted to 1985 value times four), rather than the present $8,700.

The point is that tax liability for family incomes presently begins below the defined poverty line, and the redistribution of income away from families with children because of the decline in the value of the personal deduction may be a significant contributor to the growing number of poor children. Returning money to poor families in the form of ADFC payments, food stamps, and other programs is clumsy and accompanied by a host of abuses and humiliations. It probably would be far more effective if this money had not been collected in the first place. This reform, conceptually simple but costly in terms of revenues not collected, would reasonably test the mettle of a society that claims that it is concerned about strengthening the family and the values of family life.

The panel, which spiritedly discussed nearly every subject before it, would no doubt take issue with these three items that I insist bear more study and probably action. Panel members will, however, speak in their own voices in the following chapters as do our colleagues who contributed so generously to the debate.

NOTES

1. An excellent discussion of how families are affected by changes in the tax law is to be found in Moynihan (1986: ch. 3).

REFERENCES

Moynihan, Daniel P. 1986. *Family and Nation.* New York: Harcourt Brace Jovanovich.

U.S. Bureau of the Census. 1985. *Money, Income and Poverty Status in the United States.* Washington, D.C.: U.S. Government Printing Office.

2 GOVERNMENT AND FAMILY POLICY

Senator Daniel Patrick Moynihan

In the late nineteenth century, increased awareness of the problems of industrialization and the rise in trade unionism led to a general movement for social legislation that addressed the problems of the workplace and the conditions of industrial workers. These events all helped move the issues of the workplace onto the political agenda of that period; it took a near half century and more for government to work through the reform agenda, and it is hardly finished. Nevertheless, as in Europe at the time, issues of the workplace severely tested the ability of the political system to respond to the expressed interests of the polity.

Such events are rare and significant. Indisputable data over the past twenty years suggest to me that in the last years of the twentieth century we will witness another such infrequent and important event: Something we shall call *family policy* will finally move onto the political agenda.

Family policy must be recognized as something quite different and distinct from family piety. The rhetoric of family piety not infrequently involved the proposition that government should be kept out of family matters. Events have led the polity to realize that of necessity government is involved.

This chapter was adapted from a speech delivered to the Economic Policy Council on January 16, 1986.

7

In April 1985 I had the honor of delivering the Harvard University Godkin Lectures. The subject I chose: family policy. Nearly twenty years ago, in an introduction to a paperback edition of Alva Myrdal's *Nation and Family*, I wrote, "In the nature of modern industrial society no government, however firm might be its wish, can avoid having policies that profoundly influence family relationships. This is not to be avoided. The only option is whether these will be purposeful, intended policies or whether they will be residual, derivative, in a sense, concealed ones." This proposition was clear then as now.

The effort on my part to revive the family issue in 1965 was rejected, but even so, facts inevitably drive an issue. The facts are: We have become the first industrial nation in the world in which children are distinctly worse off than adults. In 1984, according to census data, a child under age 6 was seven times more likely to be poor than was a person over age 65. Clearly a large number of poor persons exist in the United States, and they are disproportionately young.

The national reaction to the Godkin Lectures was extraordinary. Major newspapers across the country ran favorable editorials—the *New York Times, Boston Globe, Los Angeles Times, Chicago Tribune, Baltimore Sun, Miami Herald, Detroit News, Dallas Morning News, St. Petersburg Times, Tampa Tribune, San Diego Union, San Jose Mercury News, Newsday*, and small local newspapers, like the *Herkimer Telegram*. Without dissent, commentators agreed that the problem is real; they saw evidence of it in their own cities.

An account of the Godkin Lectures appeared in *The Economist*. Under the heading "Children in Poverty, America's Disgrace," the article noted that when I first raised the subject of family breakup, during the Johnson administration in the 1960s, I "got a bloody nose." So I did. Upon raising the issue again in 1985, however, *The Economist* noted I was "swiftly reinforced by a huge study," namely a joint Congressional Budget Office and Congressional Research Service study, *Children in Poverty*. This study, published in May 1985, quantified the distinct link between poverty and the dramatic change in family structure—namely, the rise in female-headed households. The authors calculated that if the proportion of children in female-headed households had not increased over the past twenty-five years, there would have been 3 million fewer children in poverty in 1983.

As I stated in the Godkin Lectures in April 1985, put simply, poverty is now inextricably associated with family structure. Year-to-year increases in poverty rates for children have been connected with various economic factors, among them severe recessions and rapid inflation. But over the past two decades, rising poverty among children has been principally correlated with the rising proportion of female-headed families.

The statistics on child poverty are known, but the essentials bear repeating. In 1984 more than one-fifth of all U.S. children were living in poverty—13.3 million poor children in a nation of considerable riches. The 1984 child poverty rate of 21.3 percent was higher than it was over two decades ago; for young black children it was the highest ever—over 51 percent.

In 1984 female-headed families represented just 16 percent of all families but accounted for almost half of all poor U.S. families. In fact, in 1984, for the first time, female-headed families in poverty outnumbered married-couple families in poverty. Children in female-headed households are the most disadvantaged: One-half of children in female-headed families are poor; two-thirds of such black children are poor; and nearly three-fourths of such children of Spanish origin are poor.

In the Godkin Lectures, I also focused on another key piece of data: Family incomes have been declining over the past decade. While average real incomes for U.S. families rose rapidly during the 1950s and 1960s, they peaked in 1973 and have been declining since. For the three decades before 1973 family incomes rose virtually every year: During that period, we never went more than three years without setting a new record.

The indicators of family disintegration show a worsening trend. The problems I identified among minorities in the mid-1960s have become general to the population of the 1980s. In 1965 I could state that "the United States is approaching a new crisis in race relations," because the number of nonwhite families with a female head had reached 21 percent. By 1984 the Census Bureau would report that for white families with children, 20 percent would be living with one parent. 1960 had been 9 percent, 1970, 10; then, of a sudden, double. In 1984 single-parent families with children accounted for more than one-quarter (26 percent) of all family groups, compared with 22 percent in 1980 and only 13 percent in 1970. Demographers

Arthur Norton and Paul Glick (1986: 16) have forecast that 60 percent of children born in 1984 can expect to live in a one-parent family before reaching age 18. David Ellwood and Mary Jo Bane (1984: 26) estimated that in 1984 one-third of white youth and three-quarters of black youth then age 17 had spent some time during their childhoods in broken families. They were projected that in ten years these proportions will likely rise to 46 percent for white youth and 87 percent for black youth.

The relation of family disintegration to the economic status of children was forecast by us over twenty years ago, but official sources of data were then painfully lacking. Now we are becoming almost overwhelmed by the data and the attention given to them.

In 1985 the Congressional Budget Office and Congressional Research Service Study provided such an official source. More recently a related study, "How Have Families with Children Been Fairing?," was released on Christmas Day by the Joint Economic Committee. It compared the incomes of two-parent families with female-headed families. It found that from 1973 to 1984 real incomes for two-parent families with children declined 3 percent (from $35,000 in 1973 to $34,000 in 1984.) For female-headed families with children—families who have only about one-third the income of two-parent families—the decline was fully 8 percent (from $14,000 in 1973 to $13,300 in 1984).

The Joint Economic Committee also found that income inequality among families had worsened; that is, the gap between the incomes of rich and poor families had widened. Over the 1967–84 period the share of all income received by the bottom 40 percent of families fell substantially, from 20 percent to 15 percent, while the share received by the upper 40 percent of families rose from 62 percent to more than 67 percent.

Government policy helped produce these results. The Joint Economic Committee study indicates that government cash transfer programs in 1984 were far less effective in alleviating poverty among families with children than they had been a decade previous. Among two-parent families with children, cash transfers reduced the number of persons in poverty by 25 percent in 1973 but by only 16 percent in 1984. Among female-headed families with children, the effectiveness of cash transfers was cut in half: Such transfers reduced poverty by 24 percent in 1973 but by 1984 they reduced poverty by only 12 percent. This decline in effectiveness should not surprise, given that the average cash transfer received by female-headed families with children declined in real dollars from $5,200 in 1973 to $3,300 in 1984. This finding is consistent with the already observed trend in Aid to Families with Dependent Children (AFDC) benefit levels— a one-third decline since 1970.

More official recognition of the family problem is coming from our metropolitan areas, A study released in December 1985 by the Greater Washington Research Center found a fifth of the residents of the District of Columbia to be poor and almost half of those in poverty living in female-headed households. Nearly one-third of all black children in Washington are poor, and they fit the description of a "persistently poor" underclass: They can be expected to remain poor for at least ten years. The study found that some one-third of the District's children are on welfare, receiving Aid to Families with Dependent Children (AFDC).

Washington's situation is not much unlike that of New York City. Forty percent of New York City's children were poor in 1982, and more than two-thirds of them were living with only one parent. With the help of a range of institutions, I was able to project that 32 percent of the children born in the United States in 1980 will find themselves on public assistance before their eighteenth birthdays. Using the same techniques, I was later able to estimate that slightly over one-half of children born in New York City, America's most important and "wealthiest" city, could expect to be on public assistance before they graduated, or failed to graduate, from high school. Again, in the familiar vein, the composition of the poor population in New York City has been changing: It is younger and increasingly dominated by women and their children.

Such statements connecting family structure with economic status can now be made without fear of reprisal. Statements on family problems have indeed become a respectable form of political rhetoric. Inaugural speeches made by top New York City officials on January 1, 1986, are evidence of this. Mayor Edward I. Koch stated that "even the most sensitive and responsible city government cannot replace the family." City Council President Andrew Stein spoke of the large number of children who today "carry with them the burdens of poverty and family disintegration." Comptroller Harrison J. Goldin cited "the feminization of poverty and ever larger number of entire families trapped in a repeating cycle of poverty for generations to come." Manhattan Borough President David N. Dinkins: "We do not accept that government is unable to prevent the creation of a permanent underclass. Our young people are our future. They are not statistics of despair."

Adding to this recognition of these problems, we now have the important recommendations put forth by the Family Policy panel of the Economic Policy Council. These focus, and appropriately so, on one key part of the equation: What can government and private institutions, particularly employers, do in response to the demands placed on working parents? These parents in the overwhelming majority are compelled financially to pursue dual roles: one in the family and the second in the workforce. A majority of mothers with children work: 70 percent of mothers whose youngest children are between ages 6 and 13; 60 percent of mothers with children between ages 3 and 5; and 50 percent of mothers of children under age 3. Some of these women are in married-couple families, but a rising number are single parents. Some 20 million children under age 13 have working mothers in this country, and 13 million of these children are under age 6. The recommendations of the Economic Policy Council make sense: Increase the supply of federally financed child care, and provide tax incentives to employers to provide such. Such are not new ideas. As an aide to Averell Harriman in the 1950s, I once recall telling Jonathan B. Bingham that from working on messages to the state legislature I had reached the point where I could type "DAY CARE CENTERS FOR WORKING MOTHERS" in a nana-second. A recent report of the House Government Operations Committee (1985) found that for low-income families receiving welfare, "the lack of safe and affordable child care can foreclose the possibility of employment, training, education, and even the opportunity to job hunt." For many of these reasons, I introduced legislation two years ago that would grant monies to states specifically to provide child care and related support services for young AFDC mothers. The Economic Policy Council has also made other useful recommendations to government: Increase the funding for preschool programs such as Headstart, and provide complete prenatal, maternal, and child health care coverage. Employers ought to be required to pay disability leaves of a certain minimum duration, as well as be encouraged to allow parents flexible work schedules and more liberal leave policies.

Focusing on parents and the workplace is critical if we are to promote the economic well-being of families. Census Bureau statistics make this clear: The decline in the real incomes of families over the past decade would have been far worse had it not been for the increased earnings of wives and of women heading households. The earnings of wives raised mean family income, reduced poverty, helped to improve family income equality by increasing the share of income going particularly to the lowest-income group of families. Thus, facilitating the role of mothers in the workforce will contribute to the economic status of families.

I have been arguing for some time now—with not overmuch success—that government has got to make better provision for those with little or no income, which is to say AFDC families. In the 1960s and 1970s, all federal entitlement programs were indexed against price inflation, with the lone exception of entitlements for children. AFDC remains the only entitlement that has never been indexed. Further, there is no national floor for AFDC payments. AFDC, Title IV of the Social Security Act, should be brought into conformity with other cash benefit programs; the federal government should set a national minimum benefit standard and index that standard to inflation. Unfortunately, there is little prospect for accomplishing this for probably yet another decade.

Still some continue to talk about it. Recently the bipartisan Committee on Federalism and National Purpose, headed by Senator Daniel J. Evans, former governor of Washington, and Virginia Governor Charles S. Robb issued a set of recommendations. Their report, *To Form a More Perfect Union*, found that "Too many of our children confront a world of limited hope and opportunity." Establishing uniform nationwide eligibility standards and minimum benefit levels for AFDC and Medicaid and increasing federal financial support for such improvements were among their main recommendations.

I was able to assure that every Democratic Party platform since 1964 (save 1972, with which I was not involved) contained a recommendation for federal assumption of the costs of such a national AFDC program. But in 1984 Vice President Mondale demurred: Since there is no money in the budget for it, there is no point in promising it. In 1980 President Carter left a budget that did not include AFDC improvements; his budget director did not want to give the administration one more easy cut.

A national standard for AFDC payments would declare a genuine national concern for our children. Its absence is the clearest example we have of a national family policy that takes the form of denying policy. Other AFDC reforms, particularly an expansion of work and training programs and programs designed to reduce the incidence of teenage pregnancy, hold promise for reducing long-term welfare dependency. These proposals—and more—are contained in comprehensive legislation, the Family Economic Security Act (S. 1194), which I introduced last year with two of my colleagues from the House, Representatives Harold E. Ford of Tennessee and Charles B. Rangel of New York.

Against the backdrop of rising poverty and rising welfare dependence, these improvements seem necessary and urgent. But there is not much hope for immediate action. Our proposed legislation is an agenda of things to do, very few of which are going to get done in this Congress or the next. But we must continue to work to raise awareness of the problem—to raise family consciousness, if you will.

Unfortunately the federal government has become substantially disabled in providing the necessary financing for such programs. Intended or not, over the past five years we have dismantled the public financing for such programs. One result: AFDC—our one program for poor children—has been cut $3.6 billion since 1981.

This year the House and Senate made progress on three proposals I offered: (1) to provide special help in finding jobs and homes to older AFDC children who age-out of foster care so that they are less likely to end up on welfare or homeless; (2) to establish a program aimed at the problems of pregnant teenagers that would provide, among other things, job counseling, child care, transportation, and the like to young AFDC mothers—and a way out of their cycle of welfare dependency; and (3) to mandate that all states providing AFDC provide such benefits to children of intact, two-parent families where one or both parents are unemployed, a requirement that represents the first national AFDC benefit standard. These three initiatives—small but important steps—were adopted by one or both houses of Congress but fell victim in the final days of the 1985 session to White House opposition and fiscal constraints.

Growing recognition and open discussion of family problems are events to be noticed. Just yesterday, the lead *New York Times* editorial referred to how, after the death of Martin Luther King, Jr., "the plight of the black family became taboo for public discussion, with dreadful consequences."

We have come far. We are more aware of family problems and have reached higher levels of inquiry. But we are doing less about those problems, and it will be a long time before we will do more. We are in a trough in social policy. But if we continue to focus attention on the data, we will be forced to think hard about what government will do when we do get the chance to act.

As I ended the Godkin Lectures: "There is that business about it being darkest before dawn. All I have ever hoped for is that this matter might rise to the level of public discourse. This seems now to be happening. If it does, the future will be different, at least some-what different, and possibly better."

REFERENCES

"Children in Poverty—America's Disgrace." 1985. *The Economist* (June): 1–7.

Congressional Budget Office and Congressional Research Service. 1985. *Children in Poverty*. Washington, D.C.: U.S. Government Printing Office.

Economic Policy Council. 1985. *Work and Family in the United States: A Policy Initiative*. A Report of the Family Policy Panel. New York: United Nations Association of the United States of America, Inc.

Ellwood,, David, and Mary Jo Bane. 1984. *The Dynamics of Children's Living Arrangements*. Prepared for U.S. Department of Health and Human Services.

House Government Operations Committee. 1985. *Opportunities for Self-Sufficiency for Women in Poverty*. Washington, D.C.: U.S. Government Printing Office.

Joint Committee on Federalism and National Purpose. 1985. *To Form a More Perfect Union*. Washington, D.C.: The National Conference on Social Welfare. December.

Maxwell, Joan Paddock. 1985. *No Easy Answers: Persistent Poverty in the Metropolitan Washington Area*. Washington, D.C.: Greater Washington Research Center.

Myrdal, Alva. 1941. *Nation and Family: The Swedish Experiment in Democratic Family and Population Policy*. Cambridge: M.I.T. Press.

New York Times. 1986. Editorial. January 15.

Norton, Arthur, and Paul Glick. 1986. "One-parent Families: A Social and Economic Profile." *Family Relations* 35 (January).

U.S. Congress. Joint Economic Committee. 1985. "How Have Families with Children Been Faring?"

3 COLLECTIVE BARGAINING'S ROLE IN THE DETERMINATION OF FAMILY POLICY

John J. Sweeney

Collective bargaining has played an important role in the determination of family policy, and today labor supports programs that can help us better deal with the often conflicting demands of work and family life in a society that is undergoing a revolutionary transformation. U.S. families are indeed going through a revolution:

Divorce rates are climbing, and fertility rates are falling;
Increasing numbers of children are being raised in single-parent homes;
Married women are entering and staying in the labor market in record numbers;
Over 40 percent of all workers are female;
Seven out of ten employed women work full-time;
Forty-eight percent of mothers with children under age 1 are now in the workforce; and
Six out of ten mothers with preschool-age children hold full-time jobs.

Despite the increase in women in the workforce, however, women remain clustered in occupations at the low end of the pay scale. Women still earn approximately 60 percent of what men earn and comprise almost 60 percent of persons in poverty. Half of all families headed by women with children fall below the poverty line.

These trends are disturbing. But it is important to recognize that working families and poor families have always had severe strains put on them. Their struggle to survive and prosper has always been a difficult one, and economic pressures have always translated into social problems for U.S. workers and their families. Keeping a family together has never been easy for working people and for poor people.

Unfortunately, the debates on family policy and issues affecting women workers all too often ignore the fact that these problems are in the workplace and not merely at home. The labor movement, however, has always supported programs that enhance workers' ability to care for and nuture their families. We have supported legislative efforts to establish minimum wages, enact child labor laws, eliminate discrimination in employment, provide income protection, and ensure adequate health care to millions of Americans. In addition, the labor movement has always supported public education, safety and health laws, and consumer legislation, all of which have the ultimate goal of making the job of raising a family a bit easier for Americans.

We have pursued these efforts because of their importance to the maintenance and strength of the U.S. family. But we have also recognized that legislative efforts are just one approach to dealing with the needs of the family. Through the collective bargaining process, the labor movement has also dealt with the problems of low- and moderate-income families. Maintaining income levels is one area in which organized labor has played a major role; ensuring decent wages for all workers has always been a priority item for us. Our success in delivering higher pay to our members is well-documented, but it is important to recognize that unions, through the collective bargaining process, have also raised the wages of all workers in U.S. society, whether they are union members or not.

In addition to efforts to ensure decent pay and eliminate the exploitation of all workers, labor has advocated specific programs targeted to certain groups in U.S. society. For example, the labor movement has been one of the most vocal and active supporters of pay equity efforts. The Service Employees International Union (SEIU) has long advocated the elimination of sex-biased wage discrimination through the bargaining process, and SEIU locals have used their strength at the bargaining table to negotiate for pay equity. Consider the following facts:

Thirty years ago only about 10 percent of mothers with young children worked outside the home, and now 45 percent of them do (in fact, more than one-half of children between ages 3 and 5 have mothers in the workforce);

In the past women's participation in the workforce followed an M-curve (they entered the labor force in their early 20s, withdrew with marriage and children, and returned when their children grew up); today the pattern of participation in the workforce by men and women is very similar;

Women's jobs are still clustered in the lower paid, less skilled occupations (80 percent of all clerical workers are women, while only 6 percent of all craft workers are women); and

The average income for women continues to be near 60 cents for every dollar of income that a man earns.

Ten years ago we bargained our first equity adjustments for clerical workers in Santa Clara County. In Contra Costa County our union recently bargained a 3 percent pay equity increase for female-dominated job titles in addition to a 5 percent general wage increase. And 30,000 California state workers in female-dominated job categories—including clerical employees, nurses, and librarians—received equity adjustments in addition to a 8 percent pay increase thanks to the efforts of SEIU Local 1000.

Our long experience with pay equity has taught us many things. We have had to fight against the notion that certain jobs are female jobs and certain jobs are male jobs. We have had to fight against the long-standing biases that established existing job evaluation systems and that pervade pay structures.

The central fact today is that most women work out of necessity. The phenomenon of women working for pin money is long past. Women who are second wage earners account for nearly 25 percent of our gross national product, and if they were paid what they should be paid, they would account for a lot more.

Challenges and legislative efforts are important components of a strategy to eliminate wage discrimination. But our successes have come mainly through the power we have exercised in wage negotiations. We have recognized that pay equity is an issue that must be dealt with at the collective bargaining table. Eliminating discrimination in wage and benefit structures and upgrading the pay of female-dominated jobs titles are important goals of all labor unions, and these are priority issues for SEIU locals. Negotiating bias-free pay structures is one of the most important contributions that organized labor can make to the U.S. family.

In addition, one of the most overriding needs for families in the United States today is the need for decent and affordable daycare. Yet decent daycare is the exception, not the rule. It is ironic that as the needs of families grow more urgent the federal commitment to providing for those needs is being eroded. In the past three years, for example, federal programs supporting child care have been cut by $10 billion. Yet affordable, high-quality child care is vital to the ability of families to maintain decent living standards. We simply cannot wait for politicians to solve this problem.

SEIU locals are emphasizing the importance of child care at the bargaining table, and we can point to some successes. For example, in May 1985 SEIU Local 285 in Boston opened an on-site day care center at Boston City Hospital. This center was the product of a joint labor/management committee on child care established previously in negotiations between the union and the employer. Union members struggled to get the center operational, and they continue to fight for high levels of funding to allow service expansion to meet growing needs.

Another SEIU local negotiated a pilot information and referral service. Local 399 finally achieved this goal after ten years of grass-roots organizing and activity on the part of its members. It is a small but important step forward.

SEIU locals in other parts of the country have attempted to bargain child care benefits, but most unions have met with limited success in negotiating employer-sponsored child care programs. Although we have met with severe employer resistance in many areas, our locals continue their efforts to bargain over this increasingly important issue.

Our ability to bargain over issues other than pay structures increases opportunities to help working Americans and their families in other vitally important ways. One point raised earlier in this chapter related to clustering of women in low-paying jobs. We will continue our efforts to upgrade the pay of these job titles, but we also must recognize that we are never going to solve the problems caused by the wage differential between men and women until we have effective training and career development programs that allow these workers to move into higher-paying jobs.

Through the efforts of our lead program, we have developed apprenticeship programs in the service sector. These programs permit workers to maintain their current jobs and still receive the necessary education, training, and accreditation to move into better-paying jobs. For example, we are apprenticing nurses aides and orderlies to become LPNs, and we are apprenticing LPNs to become RNs. These education programs range from basic efforts to the establishment of comprehensive career ladders within a workplace. They also involve joint efforts of labor, management, and local educational institutions to train, upgrade, and educate workers for the benefit of the employer and the employee.

Another important issue dealt with through the bargaining process is the issue of flexible work hours. Here flextime provisions have been negotiated in contracts to allow workers a wider range of options in scheduling their jobs and juggling the demands of their family life. SEIU locals also have bargained over parental leave policies and have attempted to ensure that workers receive a steady income during and after pregnancy.

Through our efforts at the bargaining table, we are taking steps toward establishing policies to deal with the changing workforce and work environment. Collective bargaining can provide enhanced income security, adequate benefits, and increased opportunities for U.S. workers and their families. It cannot, however, take the place of an overall commitment by U.S. society to the protection and nurturing of the family. Sad to say, this revolution in our workforce has become a political football for many who have agendas other than simply maintaining family integrity.

At the 1980 White House Conference on Families, the AFL-CIO submitted organized labor's view of the problems facing the U.S. family in the 1980s. We stated at that time that there were many unmet needs in the United States that hurt the family—unmet needs in health care, education, social services, and welfare programs, in providing on-the-job training, and in fighting discrimination. Yet in the four years since that conference, U.S. policy toward families seems to be taking giant steps backward. The past four years have seen an attack on many critical social programs enacted specifically to deal with problems that confront U.S. families.

But perhaps worse than all of the cutbacks in funding for social programs is the deadliest enemy of the U.S. family—unemployment. There is no doubt that unemployment leads directly to increased child abuse, increased wife beating, and increased divorce. Today the mismanaged U.S. economy has the potential to wreck millions of U.S. families. Unemployment means far more than the loss of the family's economic wherewithal: It destroys the family's sense of security, the parent's self-image, and often the family's esteem in the community. The stress that unemployment puts on families— often young families—can be especially decisive. Fear of unemployment is especially strong in the communities threatened by plant closings or where new technologies threaten old occupations. Against such a destroyer of human families, collective bargaining can do little beyond seeking some measure of job security or level of income maintenance for workers who are fortunate to be represented by unions.

But it does not have to be this way. We can have a society that protects families, especially mothers and children—a society that provides a decent job for everyone who wants to work and supportive services for the families of working people. We can have a society in which the economy provides decent wages to all workers, male or female, skilled or unskilled and one in which the family is a secure and protected entity.

The two major ingredients for such a society are a national will and a commitment by the national government. I believe that the national will exists, but for us to realize this kind of society, it is essential that we alter the direction of government policy being promoted in Washington today. We must return to a government of the people—a government run by the people for the common benefit of all the people not just for the benefit of an affluent few.

The family as we have traditionally known it is not disappearing. I do not believe, as do some economists, that the family was suited only for a certain type of industrial structure and that the changes brought about by twentieth-century society spell doom for the traditional family structure. Margaret Mead said it well when she noted that the family is "the toughest institution we have."

Despite the devastating effect of present economic problems on family lifestyles, U.S. workers and the U.S. labor movement will continue to fight at the bargaining table, in the halls of Congress, and in the courts for decent and humane public policies designed to assure the continued survival of the family as we have come to know it.

4 THE LEAST OF THESE

Mario M. Cuomo

Marian Wright Edelman has infused the Children's Defense Fund with her strength and vision and love and made it into one of the foremost private-sector advocates for our children and their families. She has been the soul of the CDF—an energetic, eloquent, and persistent advocate in the struggle for social justice—and everyone who cares about the millions of children in need of help and hope is indebted to Marian Wright Edelman's leadership.

I hope these words make clear my respect for her, for the CDF, for its vision and its work. But if they don't, there is one other thing that offers dramatic proof of how I feel: In order to participate in this conference I gave up good seats at Madison Square Garden for tonight's Georgetown/St. John's game—and as one who went to St. John's College, St. John's Law School, married a St. John's graduate, and has two children who went there, that's not easy. This basketball game is being billed as "*the* game of the 1980s." It's not hard to understand the excitement—what teams, what a pleasure to watch them. Chris Mullen is the all-American boy—six feet six, from a beautiful family, gifted, accomplished, a great future in front of him. For Pat Ewing, the sky is the limit; he can reach up and grab all the success he wants. The twenty to thirty young adults

This chapter was adapted from a speech delivered to the Children's Defense Fund on February 27, 1985.

on these teams are in superb condition—America's young at their best, grown straight and strong, magnificently equipped to compete.

The truth is, not all our children grow up like Chris Mullen or Pat Ewing. Some don't grow up at all. When the cheering has stopped (and win or lose we feel proud of the way these young people have performed) it will still be true that for increasing numbers of our children the possibility of college and success—of even the *chance* to compete—is becoming more remote.

These are the children many prefer to forget, the children the CDF defends and speaks for. These are the children growing up—or struggling to—against all the odds. Millions are born to mothers barely out of childhood themselves, raised in slums or rural shacks or squalid welfare hotels, sent to schools ill-equipped to teach them. Children play in streets littered with broken glass and shattered dreams, in communities where 40 or 50 percent of the adults have no jobs, where often the only successful example of free enterprise is the drug traffic that the federal government is unable—or unwilling—to interdict.

Consider, for example, the statistics presented by the Catholic bishops.in the first draft of their pastoral letter on our economy (published November 11, 1984). "At the end of 1983," the bishops wrote, "there were about 36 million Americans who, by the government's official definition, were poor. Another 20 to 30 million had so little that by any reasonable standard they were also needy." As the bishops pointed out, since 1980 the number living in poverty has increased by over 9 million people, so that "Today *one* in every *four* American children under the age of six, and *one* in every two *black* children under six, is poor." The statistics are frightening.

You don't have to endorse every part of the bishops' prescription for our economy to appreciate the scope and accuracy of their diagnosis. They have looked at our society with candor, honesty, and compassion, describing the pain and desperation of those excluded from our "shining city on a hill," those who can see it only from a distance—glittering towers they'll never live in and luxury they'll never share in. Despite the renewed growth in our economy, the numbers of the excluded continue to increase.

There are more homeless than at any time since the Great Depression. Entire families are crammed into temporary shelters and are faced each day with the brutal question of whether or not they will find a place to sleep.

At least 20 million Americans are going without enough to eat. In the words of the report prepared at the Harvard School of Public Health by a physician task force, "Hunger is a sweeping epidemic . . . now more widespread and serious than at any time in the last 10 to 15 years."

We have more single-parent families than ever before—and more women in poverty and more teenage mothers without a proper education or the prospect of a job. We have increasing numbers of children whose mental and physical development has already been stunted by poor nutrition and inadequate medical care.

No one, in fact, disputes these statistics. Even those who seem to believe that it is depressing and unduly negative to pay attention to these conditions do not deny their existence. Nor is there a great deal of political disagreement about the cause of these conditions. Most conservatives as well as liberals understand how discrimination and hunger and lack of education can twist a life and thwart it—how poverty can perpetuate itself.

What we disagree over is a solution. Some believe that words and "the free market" are enough. Last week, for example, Secretary of Education William Bennett was asked whether the federal government could do anything to promote better teaching in our schools. The Secretary answered, "Yes. One thing it can do is talk about teaching." Talk about it? In a nutshell that is the philosophy that increasingly threatens this country. It's not new, but today it's fashionable.

An active and compassionate government, the philosophy goes, impedes the evolution of society. The only way to help the poor and the weak is for government to make the rich richer and the strong stronger, and as they ascend this world's ladder of success, they'll pull the rest of creation with them. Government, the proponents of this philosophy hold, should restrict itself to preaching about "traditional values." Government should exhort people to work but not help them find jobs; it should preach the value of education but not practice the policies that extend and support educational opportunity; it should affirm the sanctity of life in the womb but not help women to feed or house or clothe or educate or care for their babies.

I am against neither preaching nor traditional values. As a matter of fact I can think of no organization in this country that does a better job of upholding and advocating *real* traditional values than the CDF, a private-sector organization that neither seeks nor accepts government support. The CDF embodies the beliefs that for half a century, from the 1930s to the 1980s, formed the basis of public policy in this country. It represents the traditional values that gave economic stability to family life, that helped parents find work and feed their children, that slashed infant mortality rates and brought a basic level of medical care to pregnant women, that created new opportunities for black and hispanic children, for the children born blind or retarded, the children in wheelchairs.

The CDF recognizes the power of preaching all these things. But it knows that families do not survive on words. It recognizes that sermons are not enough. And it recognizes as well that despite all the extraordinary efforts by all those in the private sector, depending on private charity will never be enough.

Once—not long ago—it seemed that our entire society understood this. Because we understood, we insisted that our government be committed to these traditional values, to using public policies and programs to lift people into the middle class, to help make life secure for the elderly, to care for those who often cannot survive without some degree of assistance—especially the "least of these," the children utterly dependent on a society concerned about their futures.

It is ironic, I suppose, that this long-standing consensus on government's obligation to helping improve the condition of people's lives has been attacked and eroded by those who claim to represent values that are "pro-family." Even more ironic is that the same people who trumpet the enormous strength and success of our nation— who boast of our so-called economic recovery, who deny any limits to our ability to grow larger and stronger—these same people say we are not capable of defending ourselves and at the same time caring for our children and our poor. For fifty years we did both. Generations were saved and lifted up by a government that did both. Now we are told that the best we can do is to write a tale of two cities and to hope that we find room for ourselves in the one with the swimming pools.

Think about it. At the same time that we have heard a symphony of noble words about the sanctity of the family and the dignity of motherhood and reverence for life, we have seen savage cuts in the programs that help mothers and fathers sustain their children, that educate the young, that prevent birth defects and infant diseases, that give parents the chance to earn their own bread. In an era when we are supposedly "returning to strong, time-honored American values," we have witnessed the struggle of the CDF to protect and defend the swelling numbers of abused and abandoned children, of impoverished mothers, of families without adequate food and medical care, sometimes without even a roof over their heads.

And still, some continue to say that we have no choice. Social programs don't work, they say. Or maybe they worked once—maybe they worked long enough to send generations to college, to create an enormous middle class, to give millions of us a security we never had before—but they can't work anymore. America, they say, can't afford to be both competitive and compassionate. We are no longer able to design programs that can reach people without stifling them.

More and more, love is seen as weakness and the traditional idea of a collective obligation to the frail or the old or the poor or the young as unrealistic—as an unfair redistribution of hard-won gains. For many the denial of compassion has become respectable.

But it is a philosophy that we in New York still reject. We reject it in our private sector where hundreds of groups—religious and non-religious—organize to volunteer their time and resources to help others. And we reject it in our government. Out of *compassion?* Yes, *compassion* is not a word we are afraid to use. But we do it not just out of compassion but because we believe that investing in helping the disadvantaged and those who need a start in life makes common sense—even practical economic sense. In New York, Republicans as well as Democrats understand that if we bring children into this world and let them go hungry and uneducated, if we are indifferent to the drugs and violence that surround them—and to the despair that results—then we whose children have been reared in comfort and decency will reap the same bitter harvest. We understand that we will have to pay to maintain a growing number of people at subsistence levels, to spend more on jails and police, to take money we could have used for schools and day-care centers to build prisons instead. We will live amid increasing social disorientation and in fear—with bars on our windows and in suburban enclaves walled off from the cities they surround.

And yet we know that it does not have to be like this. We know that government can do more than make bombs or pile missiles until they pierce the skies. We know that we are intelligent enough to find progressive and pragmatic ways to help people and to do so without smothering their ambitions or spending ourselves into bankruptcy. We did it for fifty years in this country—and in New York we're still doing it. We are applying old principles in new and innovative ways. Since 1983 we have put in place an array of reasonable and workable programs that are reducing dependency, not encouraging it:

Our "school to employment program" keeps teenagers in school and at the same time gives them experience in a private-sector job that will be theirs when they graduate.

Our employment assistance program and the work incentive program are all helping people get off the welfare roll and on to the private-sector payroll.

Our adolescent pregnancy prevention program is a comprehensive statewide initiative designed to deal with the growing tragedy of children having children. We call the program "new avenues to dignity" because it is built on the realization that the way to prevent teenage pregnancy is not by punishing those who have babies but by creating new opportunities and opening new alternatives.

The pregnancy prevention program is unique in a number of ways. It targets those communities with the highest rates of adolescent pregnancy and draws together a comprehensive range of services. We know from experience that no one service—whether education or counseling or health care or vocational training—is enough. Only an integrated network of support that creates opportunities leading to independence can make a difference. This includes training for a real job, a close relationship with a mentor or a peer group, proper health care and counseling.

The success of this effort requires new partnerships between government and the private sector. In selecting groups to receive grants we are choosing those deeply rooted in their neighborhoods and with extensive support of community volunteers. As we refine this program, we will continue to look to many of you here to share ideas and to help us learn how we can improve our effort.

Of course, no one program—no matter how comprehensive—can answer all the questions about how we encourage our children to seek fulfillment through education and careers, to conceive children only when they are prepared to be parents, to understand that there are other ways to assert their maturity and self-worth than by having a baby. The New York State Task Force on Adolescent Pregnancy that I created has issued its first report and touched on this problem. It makes clear that if we want teenagers to grow up to create strong families, then we must strengthen the families that these teenagers are now part of by giving the parents—or parent—work. We are doing that. We are spending more than ever before to give people the chance to live in decent housing, to ensure access to higher education, to create thousands and thousands of new private-sector jobs. We are doing it without deficits or waste, refuting those who argue it cannot be done by government with fiscal soundness and with efficiency. Indeed, at the same time that we are making these investments, we are reducing taxes. We are doing it with a principle that we believe is both practical and traditional—the principle of "family."

We believe that better than government preaching about family is government *acting* like a family, spreading benefits and burdens for the good of all, embodying that intelligent self-interest that acknowledges the simple common sense in nurturing and educating and encouraging *all* our children—the child raised in poverty as much as the one born to some degree of comfort.

Once—not long ago—this entire country believed this was the way government should act. Now we are tempted to forget. In the security of success, enjoying the benefits of an economy built by intelligent cooperation, we are asked to believe that there is nothing we can do together to feed babies or to care for the woman too old to work or to educate children trapped in ghettoes or on reservations or to find jobs for retarded people or to give some hope to a young woman alone with her baby, without a husband or a home or a future.

It's not true. It's not smart. It's not right. Our people are better than that. Our government can be better than that. We have an obligation to remind ourselves of that. And that is what the Children's Defense Fund does.

Perhaps, in a distant day, we won't need a Marian Wright Edelman and the rest of CDF to remind us of truths present in every human heart, of values so traditional they are almost instinctive—of family and compassion and love. But in the meantime, we are grateful we have CDF—grateful for its voice and example, strong and insistent, reminding us of the children whose world we are shaping even now by our love—or our lack of it. Please continue helping us not to forget the least of these.

5 THE ORIGINS, PROGRESS, AND FUTURE OF SWEDISH FAMILY POLICY

Anna-Greta Leijon

THE PRESENT SITUATION

Women in Sweden today are almost as extensively employed as men. If the present development of employment participation rates continues, both sexes will be gainfully employed to an equal extent by about 1990. This progress is a result of political determination, fundamental reforms of the education, taxation, and social benefit systems, and hard economics. Above all, of course, it is due to a disposition of women themselves to seek gainful employment.

Change has occurred within a relatively short period. Only twenty years ago, women's employment participation rate was no more than about one-third of men's, which in practice meant that a large number of married women were employed full time looking after their homes and children. A change of this magnitude in families' living patterns involves society in a major transformation that has not been without its problems.

HOW DID WE GET WHERE WE ARE?

Population Crisis was the title of an important book published in Sweden in 1934 by Alva and Gunnar Myrdal, who perhaps are better known for their activities in fields other than family policy. When

31

Population Crisis came out, population questions were often discussed in Europe, although not from the Myrdals' perspective. In Germany, Hitlerism was emerging with its demands for Lebensraum for the German people, racial purity, and the elimination of inferiors. In such a climate, it took courage to bring out a book with such a title, but the Myrdals used their book to describe the population crisis in completely new terms. Seeking explanations for the declining birthrates, they found them in poor housing, overcrowding, uncomfortable living conditions, the poor finances of young families, and the poor health of both mothers and children. This led them to put forward a number of demands covering the entire spectrum of family policy: better and larger homes, financial support for young families (that is, families with children), and improvements to health and medical care.

Population Crisis came as a warning bell in the Swedish debate on social welfare, and like so many warning bells, it had to ring for some time before any lasting and tangible results were achieved. World War II supervened, which put a temporary stop to reform measures. Recovery policy during the 1930s concentrated mainly on methods of combatting unemployment, and heavy resources were preempted by the defense sector during the war. Although a genuine program of social policy was put into effect only after the war, one step was taken in 1939, when legislation was passed forbidding employers to fire women because of marriage and childbirth. At the same time, women became entitled to three months' leave of absence in connection with childbirth, though without any financial compensation.

The cornerstone of the major postwar reforms of family policy was the basic child allowance, introduced in 1948. Maternity and child care were expanded through the establishment of special nursing centers. Free school meals were introduced. A socially based program of housing construction was carried out, although the Myrdals' ideas in this respect were not fully implemented. Statutory leave of absence for childbirth was extended to six months, though still unaccompanied by any financial compensation.

A basic characteristic of family policy (and social policy in general) under Swedish Social Democracy is its essentially universal and equal validity, irrespective of income. This important basic principle encourages solidarity about social reforms. Indeed, subsequent attempts to undermine Swedish social security have foundered on the fact that all social categories are affected by it.

Child allowances have been successively improved since they were first introduced, as has been a state-subsidized municipal housing allowance that is subject to a means test, based on the size and rent of the individual home and the number of children in the family.

Parental insurance has been gradually expanded from 1955, when it entitled parents to three months' leave of absence with compensation for loss of earnings, until today, when it offers a one-year leave of absence with nine months' full pay. Six of these nine months have to be taken in direct conjunction with the birth of the child. The remaining three can be taken at any time before the child reaches age 4; they do not carry full coverage for loss of earnings but instead carry a guaranteed benefit, which at present is about 48 kronor (U.S. $5) per day.

The past ten years have seen substantial improvements to parental insurance. In 1974 the program was also amended to allow parents to decide whether the father or mother will stay at home with the new arrival. A father is entitled to ten days' leave of absence in connection with childbirth, even though the mother is off work at the same time. Roughly 25 percent of new fathers take some portion of the leave to which they are entitled.

One of the principal aims of postwar family policy was to reduce the financial burden of young families. Since the 1970s expansion of public child care amenities has achieved new prominence. These demands for good public child care have been closely connected with demands for sexual equality, which is based on employment. People who have jobs can support themselves and live on equal terms with others. But if children cannot receive good care while their parents work, the right to work becomes illusory. The expansion of public child care took a decisive step forward in the mid-1970s, when improved state grants encouraged municipal authorities to accelerate the implementation rate. The goal was that 80 percent of all children with gainfully employed or student parents would have access to day nurseries by the early 1980s. The target has not been achieved: At present 38 percent of all preschool children have places in municipal child care, with 23 percent attending day nurseries and 15 percent receiving municipally subsidized family day care (day care in which a parent stays at home to look after his or her own child and takes care of other children at the same time).

Alternative arrangements must be secured for the numerous children for whom no places are available in day nurseries or family day care. Grandparents or private caregivers some times can fill the breach, and parents may stagger their working hours so that one parent is always at home to look after the children.

Sometimes these child care arrangements work well, but often they do not. The Social Democrats in Sweden are working so that all children above age 18 months can have places in day nurseries by 1991.

This expansion of child care took place during the decade that witnessed the most sweeping transformation of the labor market in modern history. During the 1970s great numbers of women entered the work force, encouraged in part by the 1971 reorganization of income taxation that allowed the earnings of husbands and wives to be taxed separately; this made it more remunerative for both parents to work. The recession of the early 1970s differed from previous recessions because women did not withdraw from the labor market but remained employed or registered with employment officers as jobseekers. All women fell into this pattern, including those with young children at home.

Since the 1970s the employment participation rate of all women has steadily risen. Women are not gainfully employed to the same extent as men, however. Part-time employment is widespread in Sweden, with a quarter of the entire labor force working fewer than thirty-five hours per week, and virtually all part-time employees are women. Women work an average ten hours less per week than men; If all the hours worked in Sweden were evenly shared out between everybody working, we would have something like a thirty-six-hour week.

Part-time employment has been good insofar as it has given many women the chance to remain employed even after starting a family, since women still bear the major responsibility for caring for house and children. But part-time employment has its drawbacks. The part-time employee often depends on somebody else—usually the man of the family—to make ends meet, and she occupies a weaker position in the labor market. Part-time employment is mainly confined to certain occupational categories that organizationally can adapt to less than full work days. In addition, women choose from a much narrower range of occupations than men do: Women are to be found in about thirty occupations, concerned predominantly with nursing, care, and services, while men are represented in 300 different occupations.

We also find that the better paid the jobs, the smaller the number of women doing it; the higher the status of the executive position, the smaller the proportion of women occupying it—particularly true in private enterprise. This is despite the fact that collective agreements in Sweden do not lay down special rates of pay for women, a practice abolished in 1962. Nevertheless, rates of pay for women have improved considerably in relative terms, due very much to the equitable wage policy that has been pursued by the Swedish Trade Union Confederation (LO) since the 1950s. Briefly, this policy has promoted equal pay for equal work, irrespective of the sector of employment, the profitability of the individual company, and the age or sex of the employee. Under these policies, the earnings of female industrial workers, which in 1960 equaled 70 percent of men's earnings, rose to 92.1 percent by 1982. Female industrial workers earn about 91 percent as much per hour as their male colleagues, and women in general earn 81 percent as much per hour as men. Because of their shorter working hours, women account for roughly one-third of the total wage bill.

Despite the nonexistence of separate rates of pay for women, income gaps exist between the sexes because the occupations in which women predominate (nursing and care) are generally low paid. This, of course, is connected with the fact that not very long ago these jobs were unpaid. The objective of full employment equality is still a long way off.

PROBLEMS TODAY

Sweden today faces a difficult employment situation caused in part by the economic recession that has affected the whole of the industrialized world since the late 1970s. This recession has forced us to reduce the expansion rate of the public sector in which large numbers of women have found employment.

The economic crisis also has directly affected our citizens. Young families are a highly vulnerable group, and domestic politics today focuses much attention on methods of improving conditions for young families. Our various political parties differ somewhat on the means they advocate to achieve this end, but there is widespread agreement that something will have to be done. Young families have been particularly hard hit by rising food prices and diminishing real earnings over the past six or seven years, although this has been par-tially compensated by a substantial raise (45 percent) in the basic child allowance: Since 1985 the allowance per month and per child is 400 kronor (U.S. $45), with an additional allowance for families with three or more children.

The disturbing decline in the birthrate is the subject of a long-term debate in Sweden that is somewhat reminiscent of the discussion raised by the Myrdals in the 1930s. The government has published a debate book on this subject. More and more frequently families con-fine themselves to one or two children and less often decide to have a third. Some parents may refrain from having additional children so that the living standards of the entire family are not reduced. But perhaps our society is not very child-friendly. It takes every pair of parents one or two children to discover this fact, and then parents refrain from having more children.

Another possible reason for the decline in birth rate (and one in which I firmly believe) is that women refuse to have more children. Parenthood, they find, is not as neatly shared as was expected before children arrived. The woman not only bears the brunt of keeping the home in order, doing the laundry, washing dishes, and comforting and playing with the children, but at the same time she works out-side the home to a far greater extent than her mother and grand-mother did. Husbands and fathers incur only a small share of the domestic work and child care. Another factor that helps to explain the declining birthrate is that adult relations are a great deal less stable today than they used to be: Fewer people marry, more couples live together without marriage, and the divorce rate is rising steadily. These changes in patterns of family life must have some bearing on nativity in our society.

FAMILY POLICY TOMORROW

The right family policy for Sweden tomorrow must make the cam-paign for shared parenthood a topic of renewed and intense discus-sion. Mother and father are both parents, although many people fail to accept the consequences of this relationship, especially the practi-cal, everyday ones. The debate over who is to wash the dishes is not an edifying one, but it has to take place if the traditionally weaker party in this context is not to be a perpetual loser. Everybody in a household must share responsibility, or we will never share equally in the workforce. It ought to be self-evident that both parents must assume an equal share of responsibility for children when they are small and also throughout adolescence. Unfortunately, it is not self-evident. I look forward to a society in which men and women, regardless of their positions outside the home, share responsibility for the care of both home and children. I am convinced that this sharing will enhance the happiness of many families and consequently of society as a whole.

In addition to shared responsibility at home, I recommend making working hours more flexible throughout the life cycle. Current Swedish law stipulates a maximum working week of forty hours, and we know that women predominate among part-time employees and that part-time employment increases among women when they become mothers. We also know that male part-time employees are to be found in the top age groups of the labor force, probably due to the availability of partial retirement pension.

It is also a fact that a majority of the labor force would prefer shorter working hours to a raise of wages and that many would welcome a reduction of working hours even if it was accompanied by a proportional reduction in wage. We know that preferences concerning retirement age vary a great deal: Some want to retire early, while others would rather defer their retirement beyond the basic retirement age of 65. Others may dream of taking time off to do things such as sailing round the world, taking a special cooking course in Paris, or staying at home and working in the garden for a while.

The logical response to these preferences is to make working hours more flexible throughout the life cycle—to allow workers to take time off for extended periods or every day and to allow other workers to remain in employment somewhat longer for intermittent periods. Once we acknowledge that the need for leisure varies throughout the life cycle, perhaps we can organize a savings scheme that allows everyone to save up prolonged periods of leave—a kind of working hours credit account.

Flexibility must be determined by the needs and preferences of the individual; I have little faith in cyclically modified working hours of the kind proposed by the employers' organizations. If everyone is to have more liberty than at present to choose their working hours, however, a great deal of organization will be required to make working life practical, functional, and efficient. This in turn presupposes

powerful union organizations that can safeguard employees' interests—otherwise we may very easily find that we have created a law
of the jungle that soon breaks the weakest. Choosing one's working
hours may some day prevail. If it causes more people to value shorter
working hours more highly, we may achieve the six-hour day—
which, to me, is an attractive goal to aim for.

6 CHILD CARE IN FRANCE

Olga Baudelot

France has a two-part child care system: child care facilities designed for children up to age 2, sometimes age 3, under the auspices of the Ministry of Social Affairs and Family, and the preschool system for children ages 2 to 6 under the auspices of the Ministry of Education. For many reasons—French child care history, left-wing and trade unions demands, and the increase in the number of female executives with children—child care has become an increasingly problematic issue. It is now a problem that has gone beyond the private family sphere and has reached the public authorities, who are responsible to all.

France has a long tradition of out-of-home child care. Leaving infants with wet-nurses (*nourrices*), has been a characteristic of French society for centuries and for all social classes. Making a living by keeping other women's children is deeply rooted in French social history.

Center care developed as early as the eighteenth century. *Salles d'asile*, care houses linked to poor houses and workshops, are the forerunners of present-day *écoles maternelles* and *crèches*. Care of the youngest children developed under the auspices of social welfare and health institutions, while the older ones were placed under the auspices of the Ministry of Public Instruction and linked to the development of compulsory education.

In the second part of the nineteenth century, *crèches* were established and managed by philanthropic societies, with the aim to lower child mortality and abandonment rates. Although infant mortality rates remained high and the financial conditions of the *crèches* were precarious, *crèches* were actively supported by different groups for the moral welfare of poor families.

Since 1945, with the development of the French social security and family allowances system, they became an established and growing institution. Under the Mother Child Protection Services (PMI), *crèches* were nationally subsidized and regulated by national requirements for staff qualifications, site requirements, and general procedural rules.

Since 1945 the number of *crèches* has increased. Once intended for a specific population of poor families, they are now supported by large numbers of middle- and even upper-class families. Today they are under the jurisdiction of the Ministry of Social Affairs and Family and operated mainly by municipalities.

French preschool, *école maternelle*, is a part of the national public educational system and from the beginning was widely participated in by all classes. At the end of the nineteenth century, the *école maternelle* had the same goals as the *crèches*: to protect children from poor families "from the dangers of the street." Its methods differed from the primary school by its global approach to the child and its emphasis on education not instruction. Because of the high quality of care offered by the *école maternelle*, preschool attendance rates have increased rapidly and steadily since 1945. Today almost every child from ages 3 to 6 and nearly four out of ten of children ages 2 to 3 goes to preschool. Though noncompulsory, preschool is the first step in the French public system of education and therefore under the jurisdiction of the Ministry of Education.

The present French government has recognized the importance of the child care issue and has produced guidelines for an early childhood policy. The report *L'enfant dans la vie (Child in Life)* reached the following conclusions!

Early childhood education is a highly recommended investment because children are future citizens;

The child should be considered as a whole person who deserves a place in society;

Public authorities should implement a coordinated and flexible child
   care service that connects the various educational and care facilities and promotes good health care;
The quality and the quantity of child care should be improved;
Parents should be associated with the child care service on a daily
   basis;
Operating hours should accommodate the needs of families;
Placement priority should be given to single-parent families, and
   handicapped and slightly ill children should be accepted in child
   care centers;
Innovative experiments should be subsidized, such as multi-*crèches*
(grouping several child care facilities) or parental *crèches*.

WHAT ARE THE NEEDS OF FAMILIES
AND HOW ARE THEY MET?

Women in France represent 39 percent of the labor force, and 83
percent of them work full-time. Between the two last censuses
(1975–82) the labor force participation rates for women ages 15 to
64 grew from 46 to 53 percent (see Table 6–1). That extra labor
force is mainly provided by young women ages 25 to 39 who keep
working: They don't quit, and if they do, it is for a short time.
Among them are mothers of children under age 3, which means that
they need care facilities.

Table 6–1. Women's Labor Force Participation in France.

	Percentage
By year	
1962	43.0
1975	46.0
1982	53.0
By age (1981)	
15–24	42.4
25–34	67.8
35–44	64.0
45–54	57.0
55–64	37.4
65+	2.5

Figure 6-1. Child Care Facilities and Their Clientele in France.

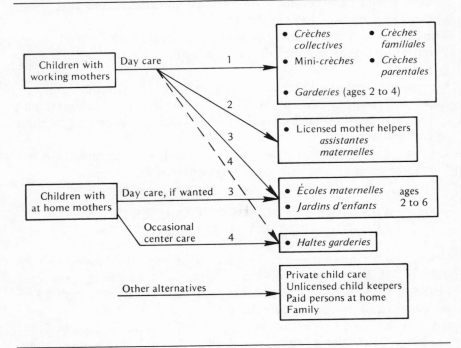

1. Licensed, wage-related, agency-operated family or center care for working parents that supervises 110,000 children annually.

2. Licensed "mother helpers" who care for about 250,000 children annually.

3. Universal benefit, when space is available, for about 250,000 children annually from ages 2 to 3.

4. These temporary center care facilities are sometimes used as part-time child care.

In 1981 roughly 2 million children were under age 3 in France, and 1 million had working parents or needed to be cared for. Figure 6-1 shows child care facilities in France and their clientele. The figures in the table show that the total amount of children kept in licensed child care centers equals 610,000. The 400,000 others are cared for either by unlicensed child care providers, who are estimated to care for around 250,000 children, by relatives, and in fewer cases by paid persons at home.

These figures give an idea who is where but are approximate. A recent research conducted by National Institute of Demography (INED) (David 1982) gives us more information. Table 6-2 shows who cares for the children of working mothers who do not attend

Table 6-2. Care for the Children of Working Mothers and Children Not Yet in Preschool.

	Total	Self-employed	Wage-earners		Living Areas		
			Part-time	Full-time	Rural	Urban	Paris District
In home							
Mother or father	23.5	69.5	31.8	7.0	29.6	23.8	14.8
Other relative	8.4	11.6	7.3	7.9	7.0	9.2	8.3
Paid person	5.9	9.5	9.1	3.8	7.0	4.7	7.4
Other	2.0	1.0	0.0	2.9	2.1	2.0	1.9
	38.8	91.6	48.2	22.6	45.7	39.7	32.4
Out of home							
Relative	18.7	5.3	18.2	22.6	19.0	22.1	9.3
Paid person	40.6	4.2	38.2	51.5	33.8	43.7	40.7
Crèche	8.6	1.1	10.0	10.3	0.7	6.1	25.9
Other	3.5	3.1	4.5	3.2	7.8	2.0	1.9
	71.4	13.7	70.9	87.6	61.3	73.9	77.8

Source: Gokalp and David (1982).

Note: These figures are percentages. Totals sometimes amount to more than 100 because they are double solutions—that is, children are kept at home by relatives *and* out of home by a paid person.

This research is a survey conducted by the National Institute of Demography. The sample consists of 4,000 women with at least one child under age 16. The total number of children is 8,941; among them 1,449 are not yet in the preschool.

preschool. It should be noted that this research points out what an important part family solidarity still plays in child care. These data are confirmed by the results of the 1982 Family Survey conducted by INSEE (National Institute of Statistics and Economic Studies) shown in Table 6–3.[1] This table shows also that day care centers are mainly used now by middle and upper classes.

Three child care modes will be discussed in more detail:

- *Preschool* because it is an extensive universal benefit unique to Europe;
- *Mother's helpers* because they are used by most families; and
- *Crèches* because they are demanded by parents but very expensive for public authorities to provide.

FRENCH PRESCHOOL SYSTEM: *ÉCOLE MATERNELLE*

French preschool is defined as an early education institution and as such represents a real social consensus. Everybody agrees that *école maternelle* is the first step of the educational system and that it is complementary to the education given by parents to their children.

In its one hundred years of existence, French preschool has developed an outstanding curriculum. As Pauline Kergomard, the pioneer theoretician, wrote in the first part of the twentieth century, in the *école maternelle* children must "learn to learn." *École maternelle* teachers have built up a corpus of experience that has been transmitted and given unity to French preschool.

École maternelle is open to every child from ages 2 to 6, if classroom space is available. Teachers (mostly women) are civil servants of the Ministry of Education, and teaching requirements are the same as those for primary school. The *école maternelle* is available throughout the country but is less readily available in the rural areas than in urban centers. The schedule is twenty-seven hours a week for six hours a day, with widespread facilities for meals and after school hours.

École maternelle is supported by either state or local funds. National subsidies cover 10 to 20 percent of total investment costs, and local authorities (communes) pay for the remaining costs. On the other hand, the state pays the main part, 88 percent, of operating

Table 6-3. Distribution of Child Care Facilities for Children under Age 3, According to Mother's Professional Status.[a]

Professional Status of the Mother	In Home		Out of Home			
	Relatives	Others	Relatives	Neighbors Friends	Mother's Helpers Childminders	Day Care Centers
Farmer	77.4	0.0	9.7	3.2	9.7	0.0
Artisan	29.3	13.3	22.3	9.0	16.0	10.1
Senior executive	12.4	18.1	8.6	8.4	36.4	16.1
Intermediary professional executive	12.5	6.2	14.5	13.7	38.5	14.7
Employee, clerk	15.1	3.1	23.3	11.2	33.8	13.5
Worker	23.9	4.8	28.1	10.9	26.8	5.5
Together	16.3	5.3	21.1	11.5	35.4	12.4

a. Children not attending preschool or cared for by the mother. Mothers are distributed according to their professional status and unemployed are not counted.

Source: Desplanques 1985.

Table 6-4. Preschool Registration Rates in France.

Year	Ages 2 to 3	Ages 3 to 4	Ages 4 to 5
1958	8.7	34.0	62.6
1968–69	12.9	55.2	87.1
1978–79	30.7	88.1	100.0
1981–82	34.8	90.2	100.0

costs (teachers' salaries). Nevertheless, the cost of *école maternelle* per day and per child is the lowest of all other teaching levels. Local authorities pay for nonteaching staff, building maintenance, school food services, busing, and school supplies. The amount provided for those expenses varies according to local policy.

Because the *école maternelle* is a public service (private preschool serves only 15 percent of the population), tuition is free. Parents pay fees for meals, before- and after-school facilities, and busing, but their contribution remains low.

Originally created for a specific population of children of poor families, the *école maternelle* has developed and generalized. This is clearly illustrated in Table 6–4.

Preschool status has changed. It is no longer a short transition toward primary school but has become a program lasting several years. Children from middle- and upper-class families attend preschool from ages 2 and 3. Preschool benefits are undeniable, and parents ask for them as a right. Studies on how *école maternelle* attendance affects compulsory school performance show that long preschool attendance lowers the repeaters in the first years of primary school.

THE 2-YEAR-OLD ISSUE

The success of the *école maternelle* with parents has created its present difficulties. A growing number of working parents realized that *école maternelle* could also provide child care and asked for both care and education. As a result of expanded preschool facilities, the attendance of the 2- to 3-year-olds increased very rapidly.

This influx of very young children created new problems. *École maternelle* buildings and programs were inadequate for the youngest children, who did not respond well to a curriculum designed for

4-year-olds. The *école maternelle* teachers felt that very young children should begin part-time social experiences but, against all expectations, were confronted with full-time attendance.

The acceptance of 2-year-old children in the present-day *école maternelle* requires preschool teachers to confront care problems such as meals, rest, relationships with parents, and so on. It also requires a reorganization of learning situations for those children. Presently, these issues are being debated among the *école maternelle* teachers.

THE "MOTHER'S HELPER" SYSTEM (*ASSISTANTES MATERNELLES*)

Mother's helpers (the new name given to at-home child care providers since the enactment of the 1978 statute)—former *nourrices* or *gardiennes*—care for young children in private agreement with parents in their homes. They are (1) licensed, which is now compulsory, and are minimally supervised by social workers; (2) unlicensed (probably the same amount of women), which is now forbidden but not repressed; or (3) licensed and on the staff of a *crèche familiale*.

In the 1970s some child psychiatrists and psychologists determined that family day care was the best substitute care. Because the best and the worst could be found on the child care market, they promoted the *crèche familiale* system and encouraged more training and control for the *nourrices*.

They also recommended that the position of child care providers be enhanced. A statute passed in 1978 aimed at increasing the number of licensed *assistantes maternelles* by giving them a minimum wage guarantee and a right to training hours.

The costs of paying for a *nourrice* are entirely paid by parents and are not charged on a sliding scale according to family income. Local authorities pay only for the few existing training programs and for the social workers who supervise the *nourrices*.

THE FAMILY DAY CARE SYSTEM: *CRÈCHES FAMILIALES*

The *crèche familiale* is family day care operated by a public agency and subsidized by the same agencies that subsidized center care.

Some twenty to forty mother's helpers comprise the care of a social agency service that collects parental wage-related fees, pays the mother's helper (less than market prices), and gives her equipment and assistance.

At the head of a *crèche familiale* is a pediatric nurse who enrolls and supervises the mother's helpers, regulates children's admissions, and organizes medical evaluations and emergency training. Often she is assisted by a secretary and educational staff.

There is presently a trend toward offering group experiences to young children in family day care and allowing time for mother's helpers to train or work at other tasks. To that end, more group sessions for toddlers, under supervision of kindergarten personnel, are organized by the *crèches familiales*. Some groups try to link family and group care. For example, a *crèche familiale* may be located in a mini-*crèche*; infants are cared for by mother's helpers who regularly visit the mini-*crèche* with the children, who become acquainted with staff members and then switch to the mini-*crèche* when they grow older.

The investment costs for a *crèche familiale* are not very high, because a *crèche familiale* is usually located in a house or apartment. Operating costs are about 30 percent lower than those of center care. About 40 percent of costs are paid by local authorities, 20 percent by the Family Allowance Fund, 38 percent by parents, and 2 percent by others. Parental contributions to the operating costs are higher than they are in center care. With the 1983 law of decentralization, local authorities (departments) have the financial and administrative responsibility of child care.

DAY CARE CENTERS: *CRÈCHES COLLECTIVES*

Crèches and mini-*crèches* are centers open to children ages 2½ to 3 whose mothers work. Fifteen children may be cared for in houses or apartments (mini-*crèches*), or sixty to eighty children may be cared for in specific institutional surroundings. The *crèches collectives* are organized to accommodate working parents; they are open twelve hours a day and at least eleven months a year. Staff members have various qualifications, including paramedical training; the head is a pediatric nurse.

Crèches are administrated by local authorities (73 percent are managed by municipalities or districts) or by private nonprofit associations. They are available in towns, and half are located in the Paris district (31,805 spaces against 69,280 for the whole country), which is the only district where a significant percentage of children are kept in *crèches.*

Even if their number is far from sufficient, it has grown rapidly: Fifty-eight percent of the *crèches* were opened within the last ten years. They are now well established and generally accepted by parents.

But their cost is heavy for local administrations, which makes it impossible for poor municipalities to underwrite them. National and regional subsidies account for 40 percent of building costs, Family Allowance Funds for another 40 percent, and the remaining 20 percent by the managing authorities (usually municipalities). There is no state subsidy for operating expenses, and therefore the manager pays 50.5 percent of them, the Family Allowances Fund 19.5 percent, and others 4.3 percent. Parents pay wage-related fees, which amount to 25.7 percent of the total expenditure.

Crèches were once a closed world that was managed by medical personnel obsessively concerned about protecting babies from germs. They have since transformed their relationships with parents and children. Parents are now welcomed and tend to be treated as partners who are encouraged to participate. Slightly ill or handicapped children are now accepted.

Staff view children more as persons than bodies and provide them with a stimulating educational environment. *Crèche* staff now are early childhood professionals and have discovered that their work

Table 6-5. Child Care in France, 1981.

Type of Day Care	Number
Day care centers	1,139
Family day care homes	539
Mini crèches	105
Parental crèches	6

Note: 700 out of the 1,790 crèches are in the Paris district.
   72.8 percent are managed by local authorities (municipalities).
   12.3 percent are managed by private nonprofit associations.
   11 percent are managed by districts (departments).

can be valuable and interesting. Those professional transformations have been made by staff members themselves and by the increased responsibilities assumed by parents. Parental pressure for more *crèches* is steady, and their reputation is increasing among the middle and upper classes. See Table 6–5.

THE COST QUESTION

Quality child care is expensive because young children need numerous and qualified personnel. Local authorities are often reluctant to undertake those expenses: Male politicians often believe that child care is only a women's issue; after all, women have managed by themselves for such a long time.

But it is not fair to take into account only costs and not benefits. Benefits certainly exist: A market economy would not have supported child care such a long time if it derived no benefits from it. Child care has freed a million women to work and allowed 500,000 others to make a living out of child care. These women are consumers and taxpayers. In addition, there are social benefits to be derived from child care and preschool:

Family policy benefits because young couples are better able to achieve their living goals.

Demographic policy is affected because family planning is made easier.

Public policy toward women benefits because they can achieve independence outside the home.

Social policy benefits because cultural and educational inequalities are reduced between children.

Health policy benefits through better preventive medical supervision and sanitary education.

These are valuable achievements.

NOTES

1. For the first time in France, the 1982 census and its complement, the National Family Survey, asked questions on schooling and child care. This emphasizes the interest of public authorities in these issues.

2. State expenditures per day and per child are lower for the *école maternelle* than for primary school, compulsory secondary school, *lycées*, and universities.

REFERENCES

Bouyala N., Roussille B. 1982. *L'enfant dans la vie (Child in Life)*. Paris: La documentation francaise.

Desplanques, Guy. 1985. *Modes de garde et scorrisotion des jeunes enfants*. Paris: National Institute of Statistics and Economic Studies.

Gokalp, C., and M.G. David. 1982. *La garde des jeunes enfants (Child Care for Young Children)*. No. 161. Paris: Population et Société.

7 MATERNITY, PATERNITY, AND PARENTING POLICIES
How Does the United States Compare?

Sheila B. Kamerman

THE NEW REALITY FOR WOMEN AND THEIR BABIES

Most of us are familiar with the dramatic increase in the labor force participation rates of women during the last two decades, particularly the rise in rates for women with young children. There is increased awareness, also, that fewer women leave their jobs when they become pregnant or remain away from work for very long even after they give birth. What is not known is the actual rate of labor force participation rates for women with infants (babies under age 1 year) and the astonishing growth in these rates over the last decade.

The new reality for most working women today involves remaining in the labor force despite pregnancy, childbirth, and child caring and rearing responsibilities. Census data, summarized in Table 7–1, show a steady increase in the proportion of recent mothers ages 18 to 44 (the prime child-bearing years) in the labor force. Labor force participation rates (LFPR) for women who had a baby within one year of the survey increased from 31 percent in 1976 to 38 percent in 1980 and to 47 percent in 1984 — a more than 50 percent increase in eight years (U.S. Bureau of the Census 1985). Although all the women interviewed had had a child within the previous year, some had infants that were only a few weeks old while others had babies who were almost 1 year of age. By age group, 32 percent of recent

Table 7-1. U.S. Women Who Gave Birth in the Last Year and Percentage Who Were in the Labor Force, 1976, 1980, 1983, 1984 (*number in thousands*).

Age of Woman and Survey Year	Number of Women	Percentage in Labor Force
Ages 18 to 44		
1984	3,311	46.7
1983	3,625	43.1
1980	3,247	38.0
1976	2,797	30.9
Ages 18 to 29		
1984	2,375	44.5
1983	2,682	42.4
1980	2,476	38.2
1976	2,220	31.8
Ages 30 to 44		
1984	936	52.2
1983	942	45.1
1980	770	37.3
1976	577	27.6

Source: U.S. Bureau of the Census, Current Population Reports.

mothers ages 18 to 29 were in the labor force in June 1976, compared with 45 percent in 1984. Similarly, among those ages 30 to 44, 28 percent were in the labor force in 1976, while 52 percent were in 1984. See Table 7-1.

New data from the Bureau of Labor Statistics reveal that almost half (48 percent) of all women with children under 1 year of age and half (49.4 percent) of all married women with children of that age were in the labor force in March 1985 (Hayghe 1986: 44). In 1975 the rate for all women was 31 percent and for wives, 29 percent. Within the last decade the labor force participation rate for married women with children under 1 year of age has increased by an astonishing 70 percent. More than 70 percent of employed women are in the childbearing years, and 80 percent of these are likely to become pregnant during their working lives. Unfortunately, recent national data on the percentage of pregnant women who worked through all or most of their pregnancies are not available, but several nonrepresentative studies suggest that the rate is very high and still rising.

Most physicians believe that women need about six to eight weeks after childbirth to recover physically and to get beyond the period when they are particularly vulnerable to disease; this is the period of maternity "disability." Most experts in child development believe that for some months after birth, children and their parents are especially needy of a close relationship with one another.

My colleague Alfred J. Kahn and I carried out research at Columbia University that examined the experiences of working women with young children in the United States, the policies of employers and the experiences of their employees, and existing state and federal policies. This research discloses how inadequate the situation is in the United States, especially compared with the experiences of other countries in dealing with pregnancy, childbirth, and the parenting of new babies—experiences that underscore that inadequacy even more and illustrate what an appropriately responsive policy might look like.

THE SITUATION IN THE UNITED STATES

To the extent that maternity or parenting benefits (a job-protected leave at the time of childbirth and a cash benefit that replaces all or a portion of earnings lost while on leave) exist in the United States, they do so as a consequence of either state-mandated temporary disability insurance (TDI), collective bargaining agreements, or voluntarily provided employee benefits. The only relevant federal legislation, the Pregnancy Disability Act of 1978 (PDA), requires that pregnant employees be treated the same as employees with any temporary disability. This has been interpreted to mean that women employed in firms providing short-term sickness or disability leaves and insurance replacing all or part of their pay also have the right to paid leaves at the time of pregnancy and childbirth (and that women employed in firms providing health insurance benefits must be covered to the levels provided in the policies for pregnancy and maternity medical costs also).[1] It does not mean, however, that all employers must provide disability insurance or even paid sick leaves—only that if they do they cannot exclude pregnancy and maternity from coverage.

Similarly, under the PDA legislation all states providing short-term or temporary disability insurance protection for workers in the state must cover pregnancy and childbirth also, but all states are not required to pass such laws. Indeed, none has since the PDA was passed; the most recent TDI law was passed in Hawaii in 1969.

No federal legislation now guarantees job-protection to those away from work (on leave) because of short-term, non-work-related disabilities. The PDA is mistakenly assumed by many in industry and in society at large to have led to almost complete maternity disability coverage of women employees—to guarantee them a job-protected leave and ensure the replacement of at least some portion of their lost wages for some period of time around childbirth, usually up to eight weeks for a normal delivery. The reality is very different.

State Temporary Disability Insurance (TDI)

Five states (California, Hawaii, New Jersey, New York, and Rhode Island) as well as Puerto Rico and the railroad industry have TDI laws requiring employers to cover their workers against the risk of non-work-related disabilities under a plan that pays a benefit replacing about half the worker's wage to a maximum, usually for a period not to exceed twenty-six weeks (thirty-nine in California). TDI benefits expire either when the employee is no longer disabled or when the employee becomes eligible for federal disability insurance under social security or for benefits under company supplementary long-term disability insurance. Some companies' long-term plans come into effect after brief periods, such as two months. In 1985 the maximum benefits in the five states ranged between $145 and $224 weekly, replacing about half the wage—or more—for most female workers. The duration of TDI benefits for maternity disability in these same states averages between six and ten weeks. The states with TDI coverage account for about one-quarter of the private employment wage loss for sickness in the United States and include about 22 percent of the total U.S. labor force.

Employer-Provided Benefits

For sickness and short-term disability benefits most members of the labor force depend on employer or supervisor benevolence or on sick pay or disability fringe benefits plans provided by the company (on its own initiative or through a collective bargaining agreement). Most large companies with such plans include both salaried and hourly workers.

National data on what employers provide or what employees receive are far more limited concerning this benefit than for health insurance or pensions. There are some data for large and medium-size firms, and there are estimates of employees' coverage. In 1981 about 57 percent of private wage and salary workers were estimated to have such coverage (Price 1982: 15–19; 23–29). This figure includes workers with only sick leave benefits as well as those with private or state disability insurance. Of all those with some protection, some 38.7 million persons actually had insurance plans that provided partial wage replacement after a three- to five-day wait and usually lasting for up to twenty-six weeks. The remainder simply had sick pay eligibility that tended to range between six and fifteen days.

These data, along with those reported by the Bureau of Labor Statistics in its survey of large and medium-size firms, tend to overstate the extent of protection against such risks because they are biased toward big firms and because they include somewhat disparate types of protection. Thus, for example, although most employers who provide disability insurance also have sickness benefits, most companies that provide sickness benefits do *not* provide short-term disability coverage. As a result, for workers in these companies, income protection (and job protection, where it exists) is generally for a much briefer period—usually less than two weeks (Price 1982, 1984).

A 1981 Columbia University survey of a random sample of 1,000 companies (260 responses) found that coverage was much less extensive than popularly believed (Kamerman, Kahn, and Kingston 1983). Including states that have TDI, only half the private sector workers are covered by some form of disability or sickness benefits that provide income replacement for six to eight weeks at the time of a normal childbirth. Because this survey, too, was somewhat biased toward medium and large firms, and because we found (as others have) that "generosity" of benefit coverage was highly correlated with the size of the firm, and because women are more likely to work for small firms, a more accurate coverage estimate would probably be that less than 40 percent of working women have income protection at the time of maternity that will permit them a six-week leave without severe financial penalty.

Although most working women have some unpaid, job-protected, time-off at the time of childbirth—which was an important accomplishment of the 1970s—these policies are still quite modest also. (There are no precise national statistics.) This survey found that most working women are permitted to take two to three months off, including, where provided, the paid disability leave. Many small employers, however—particularly those in states with no TDI—permit less. Job protection sometimes is a matter of formal policy but often is informal and discretionary. Large firms provide six months leave, with a very few permitting up to one year, including the period of disability. Most working women in the United States cannot afford to stay out this long if the leave is unpaid.

A national survey of the maternity and parental leave policies of the leading 1,000 industrial and 500 financial service companies was carried out in 1984 by Catalyst, a national nonprofit organization concerned with enhancing career and family options for employees in the corporate sector.[2] Of the 384 companies that responded to the questionnaire, 308 or 80 percent provided short-term disability insurance coverage for pregnancy and maternity (Catalyst 1986).[3] Among the 320 companies reporting the length of maternity-related disability leave taken by their female employees, 63 percent reported five to eight weeks and 32 percent reported nine to twelve weeks, the maximum period indicated. Fewer than 5 percent reported less than five weeks as the average length of disability leave taken.

About half the Catalyst respondents offer women additional unpaid leave—usually labeled "personal leave" but sometimes called "parental" or "child care" leaves—and almost one-third offer it to men. Among firms providing such a leave, most by far give between two to six months; about half offer two or three months and half four to six. Of the 30 percent of the respondents offering men an unpaid leave, more than half permit the same two to six months. The Catalyst survey found few differences in the leave policies for women managers compared with nonmanagers.

The Columbia University survey found that about 25 percent of firms permit men time off for parenting, not much less than the Catalyst survey given the larger number of small and medium firms studied. One major difference between the two surveys, however, is that the Catalyst survey found that men and women were given the same amount of time off, while the Columbia survey found a very different pattern. Paternity leaves were overwhelmingly limited to a few days—or at most two weeks—in the firms providing them, usually as personal leave. Unpaid leaves for women were often classified as unpaid disability leaves and therefore covered a significantly longer period. Men most likely to take a postchildbirth leave took time off to be with a wife during childbirth, to help her come home from the hospital, to take care of older siblings during the first few days after childbirth, or to help in the first few days at home adjusting to a new baby. Male employees who actually took a significant amount of time off in order to actively participate in child care and parenting remain very rare. What most male workers say they want and do not have is the right to take off a few days—at most two weeks—without losing pay or being stigmatized. Paternity leaves are still more of a media issue in the United States than an employee benefit reality.

Even though Catalyst reported on the policies of leading firms, their health care provisions seem astonishingly limited. One interesting finding of both studies is that the vast majority of women employees who take maternity-related leave stay away from work for a remarkably brief time—usually less than three months. Surveys that ask female employees for the optimal length for postchildbirth leaves report that most responses are quite modest—between three and six months.

By the standards of major industrial societies and in relation to what workers need, current U.S. policies are inadequate. Most working women have no right to a paid maternity disability leave at all (beyond a few days), and none have a right to a paid leave that goes beyond a brief period of "disability." No firm and no state provides for a paid maternity-related leave that lasts more than an absolute maximum of twelve weeks, and most provide far less or none at all. Generous, leading employers permit parents to take unpaid time off for parenting for about six months and in a few instances one year; but several firms do not promise that the same or comparable jobs will be waiting when longer leaves are taken, and few employees take full advantage of them because they cannot afford the income loss. At least one-third of all working women have no right to an unpaid but job-protected leave that covers the full period of disability.

Current court challenges are seeking to determine whether the right to a disability leave after childbirth may specify job protection. Most firms today guarantee women returning from a leave a "comparable job," but the definition of "comparability" is increasingly debated even for brief leaves.

Fourteen companies provided adoption benefits in 1980, and eighteen in 1981, often at a level comparable with that for natural parents. Not only is this coverage available to a minute portion of the labor force, but the benefit relates to adoption costs and does not cover leaves.

Finally, an issue of equity emerges where these benefits are concerned. For most working women, whether or not they have any kind of job and income protection at the time of childbirth is a function of where they live as well as where they work. Women who work in states with TDI have at least a minimum floor of protection. Other women depend on what their employers provide voluntarily, and most employers, as I have indicated, do not provide very much in the way of income-protected, job-guaranteed leaves.

HOW DOES THE UNITED STATES COMPARE?

The United States is unique among more than 100 other countries (including almost all the advanced industrialized countries and many less developed ones) in having no national legislation that guarantees that a woman who is not working because of pregnancy and childbirth will have (1) the right to a leave from work for a specified period of time; (2) protection of her job while she is on leave; and (3) a cash benefit equal to all or a significant portion of her wage (Kamerman, Kahn, Kingston 1983). Although most countries provide these benefits through national health insurance and include full medical insurance coverage, sixteen countries have such benefits without offering health insurance. Various policy instruments other than health insurance have been used to provide maternity and parenting benefits, including unemployment insurance (Canada and Austria), a special maternity benefit (Israel), parent insurance (Sweden), an employment benefit (Britain), and a benefit combining health insurance and mandated employer provision (Federal Republic of Germany).

European countries provide a minimum three months' paid maternity leave (the Federal Republic of Germany provides six and one-half months, and Sweden, one year, of paid leave), and the modal European pattern is about *six months'* paid leave and often an additional one year of unpaid leave. All these leaves involve job, pension, and seniority guarantees.[4] In a growing number of countries, including Norway, Sweden, Denmark, and Finland, all or part of the leave is a *parental leave* and can be used by fathers or mothers. In several others even if the paid leave is still a maternity leave, the unpaid supplementary leave is a parental benefit. In addition, several countries are now legislating *paid sick-child care leaves* for working parents to enable them to stay home to care for an ill young child, without losing pay — or their job. In most countries, adoptive parents can qualify for these benefits, too. Finally, there is a growing trend in Europe for postchildbirth leaves for fathers as well as mothers for at least some portion of the leave. A few brief illustrations illustrate the types of parental leave policies in place in other countries.

Sweden

For the first twelve months following childbirth, working parents have a right to a paid job-protected leave from work. The parent insurance benefit is a cash benefit that replaces for nine months 90 percent of the wage of the parent who is on leave, up to the maximum wage covered under social security in Sweden. A fixed minimum benefit is available for the remaining three months. (A nonworking mother also would be entitled to a minimum cash benefit during the year, but very few mothers are nonworking.) Parent insurance can be used to cover a complete leave or can be prorated to permit part-time work by either parent, for full pay, until the nine months of pay is used up. Thus a working mother might take off three months completely. She and her husband might then each work half-time for six months, sharing child care between them; or they might each work three-quarters time for six months, without significant pay loss.

In addition, Swedish parents have the right to take an unpaid but fully job-protected leave until their child is eighteen months old and to work a six-hour day (without additional financial compensation) from the end of the parental leave until their child is eight years old. All working parents are also given the right to a paid sick leave to care for an ill child at home for up to sixty days a year, if it is medically necessary.

France

Employed women are guaranteed the right to a job-protected leave of six weeks before and ten weeks after childbirth, with full wage replacement. An additional unpaid, job-protected leave is available to either parent for up to two years in companies with 100 or more employees; low-income parents may qualify for a cash benefit during this time.

Federal Republic of Germany

Women are entitled to a six-month leave (six weeks before childbirth, four and a half months after) with the same or a comparable job guaranteed on return to work. A "sickness insurance" benefit is paid by the social security system at a flat rate equal to about the average wage for women workers. In addition, employers are required to supplement this benefit to cover the woman's full wage for the first fourteen weeks. An unpaid, job-protected parental leave is also available for one year following the end of the paid maternity leave. The West German benefit is the oldest paid maternity leave and was first instituted in 1884 as part of the initial establishment of social security in Germany.

Italy

There is a mandatory maternity leave for working women for two months before childbirth and three months after. The cash benefit is provided as a social insurance benefit and replaces 80 percent of prior wage. An optional supplementary leave is available for six months with full job protection but is paid at the rate of 30 percent of wages.

CONCLUSIONS AND RECOMMENDATIONS

As more U.S. women remain in the labor force despite pregnancy and childbirth, the demand for policies that assure women time off with job and income protection at the time of pregnancy and child-birth—and that assure employees who are new parents similar protection as they adjust to becoming parents—is growing and will continue to do so. There has been some increase in governmental and employer responses to this demand, but thus far these developments have been modest.

If parental leave policies such as these exist in other countries, what kinds of policies might be possible in the United States? Pregnancy happens infrequently in a woman's life and lasts a very short period of time. Essential elements of maternal/parental policies include health care insurance, job-protected leaves, and some form of income protection. A realistic approach that would provide a minimum level of benefits and protection could look something like this:

1. Extend public programs to ensure health insurance (and thus coverage of physician and hospital costs) for employed women whose employers provide none and who are not covered as dependents under another plan. These women now tend to fall in the gap between women working for employers with good benefits and those eligible for Medicaid;

2. Enact federal legislation specifically addressing pregnancy and maternity disability leave, giving the forty-five states without temporary disability insurance (TDI) an incentive to offer some basic *floor* of protection for working women;

3. Expand the concept of disability to include a definition of "disability" at the time of pregnancy and maternity as fourteen weeks, with full wage replacement up to a specified maximum and job seniority and benefits guaranteed;

4. Mandate employers to provide a paid, job-protected, short-term disability leave to all employees, when medically certified;

5. Provide a supplementary parenting leave, following disability leave, until a child is six months old. This could add a three- to four-month unpaid parenting leave (for either parent) to the eight- to fourteen-week paid disability/maternity leave;

6. Encourage employers to allow female employees a phased-in return to work after childbirth and to give employees with very young children the choice of working part-time without loss of seniority and fringe benefits.

These options may appear to be generous, but they offer considerably less than what the majority of industrialized countries provide for working parents. These policies could play an important role in alleviating part of the current infant care crisis. The tremendous shortage of quality child care arrangements available in the United States today is most severe in infant care, which is the most demanding care to provide and the most expensive for parents to buy. Nevertheless, in the United States, unlike in any other industrial country, there is a high incidence of very young infants less than two months old being placed in child care programs, most of which are of poor quality. Paid parental leaves would eliminate some of the need for out-of-home infant care. These leaves are *not* a substitute for infant care programs but are rather an essential component of any country's infant care policy.

There are costs involved in providing these policies, and today there is great reluctance in Congress as well as in much of the corporate community to implement new programs that will incur additional costs. Though the economic constraints are real, these policies are exceedingly important to the well-being of our nation's children and to the productiveness of today's—and tomorrow's—labor force. In the past, major labor market changes such as the forty-hour work week or paid vacation time seemed equally impossible and expensive to make, yet these changes have become fully accepted. Maternity and parental leaves and benefits must also become an integral part of social and employment policies. Employers must begin to realize that these issues affect their male and female employees, their managers and secretaries alike. Maternity and parental leaves and benefits must be seen not as extraneous issues but as fundamental workforce issues.

NOTES

1. A significant number of working women, especially young women, are still not covered by health insurance where they work or as dependents.
2. Like the Columbia University survey, the Catalyst survey had a response rate of 26 percent.
3. The inconsistencies between percentages reported here and some reported in articles on the Catalyst survey occur because Catalyst computed percentages

based on the number of respondents to each item but we computed percentages based on the total number of respondents to the survey.
4. For a summary of European and Canadian developments, see Kamerman (1985). For a detailed analysis of the policies in twelve countries, see Kamerman (1980). For a worldwide overirvew, see *Women at Work* (1984).

REFERENCES

Catalyst. 1986. "Report on a National Study of Parental Leaves." New York: Catalyst's Career and Family Center.

Hayghe, Howard. 1986. "Rise in Mothers' Labor Force Activity Includes Those with Infants." *Monthly Labor Review* 109 (2) (February): 43–45.

Kamerman, Sheila B. 1980. *Maternity and Parental Benefits and Leaves: An International Review*. New York: Columbia University Center for the Social Sciences.

_____. 1985. "Time Out for Babies." *Working Mother* 8 (9) (September): 80.

Kamerman, Sheila B., Alfred J. Kahn, and Paul W. Kingston. 1983. *Maternity Policies and Working Women*. New York: Columbia University Press.

Price, Daniel B. 1982. "Cash Benefits for Short-term Sickness." *Social Security Bulletin* 45 (9) (September): 15–19.

_____. 1984. "Cash Benefits for Short-term Sickness, 1978–81." *Social Security Bulletin* 47 (8) (August): 23–28.

Silverman, Phyllis. 1985. "Maternity/Parental Leave Policies: Strategic Planning for a Changing Work Force." *New Jersey Bell Journal* 8 (2) (Summer): 33–40.

U.S. Bureau of the Census. 1984. *Fertility of American Women: June 1983*. Current Population Reports, ser. P-20, no. 395. Washington, D.C.: U.S. Government Printing Office (report prepared by Carolyn C. Rogers). Updated.

Women at Work, no. 2. 1984. Geneva, Switzerland: International Labour Office.

8 PAINTING THE CHILD CARE LANDSCAPE
A Palette of Inadequacy and Innovation

Dana E. Friedman

Since 1983 it has been difficult to pick up a newspaper or magazine and not find some mention of child care—whether in the more expected sources such as *Working Mother* or *Ms.* or in newly concerned periodicals such as *Forbes, Business Week*, or the *Wall Street Journal*. Some of the news is good, and some bad. In February 1984 thirty-four magazines carried stories about child care as the result of the efforts of a media coalition organized by the Child Care Action Campaign. This coverage focused on the need for child care and how difficult it is to find, afford, or applaud. Stories headlined the problems of abuse, liability, infectious disease, and guilt. Some articles, however, offered a glimpse of the innovation that inspires advocates and consumers to persist in the use of day care services. This coverage publicized corporate involvement, intergenerational day care, child care for sick children, and the increased involvement of fathers in childrearing. The child care picture that has been painted is one of inadequacy and inefficiency with splashes of innovation and excellence.

This dissarray persists at a time of unprecedented need for child care. Parents need child care if they are to work and support their families. By March 1985, 53.5 percent of mothers (both married and unmarried) with children under age 6 were in the labor force, and 49 percent of mothers with children under age 3 were working (U.S. Bureau of Labor Statistics 1983). The parent in job training or in a workfare program also needs child care. According to a June 1982 study by the Center for Population Studies, 26 percent of nonworking women with children under age 5 said that they would seek employment if child care were available at a reasonable cost. Among unmarried mothers, 45 percent said they would seek employment if they could find child care (U.S. Bureau of the Census 1982). The teenage parent who wants to finish school needs child care services also.

Nonworking parents may seek child care as an enriching experience for their children. The parents of children who have been abused or neglected need child care for protective reasons. For those whose children have special needs, child care is a form of therapy and respite care.

The needs span all ages of children. Infant care is critical because large numbers of working women have no maternity leave coverage or choose to take little time off from work after childbirth. Preschool care is in demand because of the rapid growth in the numbers of children ages 3 to 6 whose mothers work and because of the growing number of parents who think the experience is important for their children whether or not mothers are working. In 1984 there were 21.2 million children under age 6. This population is expected to increase by 17.2 percent between 1980 and 1990 (U.S. Bureau of the Census 1984). Nearly half of these preschoolers live in households where the mother is working. For one-third of all school-age children between ages 6 and 13, child care also is needed between the school's closing and the parent's return home from work.

WHERE ARE CHILDREN CARED FOR?

Contrary to popular belief, most preschoolers are not cared for in day care centers. An estimated 15.8 percent of working mothers rely on group child care arrangements, and about 6 percent of this group care is provided by nursery schools. About 22 percent of children of working parents are cared for in a family day care home where a neighborhood woman takes care of up to six children in her own home (U.S. Bureau of the Census 1982). About 5.5 percent of children are cared for in their own homes.

A significant portion of parents, perhaps half, rely on care within the family. Care by relatives may include grandparents and siblings;

it may also include parents who have arranged staggered work hours because relatives may not live close by or are working themselves, or because smaller family size makes siblings less available.

Many parents rely on a patchwork of programs that cuts across program types. The 1982 census found that 17 percent of mothers relied on more than one arrangement each week. Among fathers who are the primary caretaker, 28 percent used multiple forms of care each week.

The type of care used is likely to depend on the age of the child and the income and education level of the parents. Generally, younger children (less than age 3) are likely to be cared for by relatives, in-home providers, or family day care providers, while a higher percentage of children ages 3 through 6 will be served in larger group settings (day care centers, nursery schools, and prekindergarten programs). According to Sheila Kamerman (1983: 36) of Columbia University's School of Social Work, "Enrollment rates of children in preschool programs [center-based situations] are significantly higher when mothers have larger incomes and more education. Fifty-three percent of three to four year olds in families with median or higher incomes attended a preschool program in 1982 as contrasted with only 29 percent of those in lower-income families." Because center-based arrangements are more expensive than family day care programs, what seems to be developing is a two-tiered system: one for the affluent using high-quality, expensive centers and "nannies," and one for the working class families paying for low-quality centers and family day care homes, with another segregated set of services reserved and subsidized for the poor.

What is important to understand about these figures is that data about child care are about as inadequate as child care itself. The primary source of data is the *Current Population Survey* conducted by the U.S. Bureau of the Census, but its data are limited by its definition of child care and its lack of consistency with other child care surveys: For instance, a child care arrangement is counted only if the "primary or secondary care arrangements are used for the youngest child under 5 years, and only while the mother is working" (Papageorgiou 1986: 8). According to Mary Papageorgiou (1986: 8) of the Center for Statistics in the Department of Education, this definition can exclude older siblings who are in different forms of care, those who attend nursery school but not as a primary or secondary arrangement, and those in care regardless of whether their mothers work.

The reports of current day care and preschool enrollments are not indications of preference. For instance, we know very little about what parents would choose for their children given an adequate supply of care in a variety of forms. Even with an imperfect assessment of day care need, use, or preference, however, there is some knowledge about how the child care market works and the requirements of adequacy:

1. Child care should be *available* to satisfy a variety of needs;
2. It must be *accessible* so that parents can find what is available;
3. It should be *affordable* so that parents can pay for what they find; and
4. It should be of high *quality* so that parents are satisfied with what they can afford.

AVAILABILITY

Programs have different settings, auspices, and activities. The center-based programs might include church- or corporate-sponsored centers, Head Start programs, and kindergartens and nursery schools. Some of the funding for these programs may be available from government sources.

Title XX of the Social Security Act went into effect in 1975, and today it is the largest source of direct federal support for child care. A range of social services can be funded under Title XX, but child care is the only service that does not have a separate program providing additional federal support. In 1981 approximately $707 million of Title XX monies were spent on child care. That same year, Title XX was amended to become the Social Services Block Grant, which was designed to allow states greater flexibility in programming and to improve the effectiveness of the overall delivery of social services. States were also no longer required to provide 25 percent matching funds in order to receive federal dollars. As a result, thirty-two states cut their funding levels for Title XX services, and the federal share decreased from $3.1 billion to $2.4 billion.

By 1983 child care funding under Title XX was reduced to $623 million. An additional $200 million that had been specially earmarked for child care was eliminated as were special provisions for training caregivers. About twenty-four states reduced the amount of training dollars available to child care workers, thirty-three states lowered their licensing standards, and thirty-two cut back on the child care staff required to enforce the licensing standards that remained in effect.

Some states began providing child care subsidy to low-income populations through the Title IV–A Work Expense Allowance, which is part of Aid to Families with Dependent Children (AFDC). Beneficiaries under this program are not required to use child care programs that comply with licensing standards. Working parents may deduct up to $160 per month, per child from their earnings before their income is assessed for this AFDC grant. This maximum child care expenditure, however, may not reflect the actual cost of care; more important, it may limit parents in their choice of care and in their access to their preferred form of care—or even good care generally. In some cases, parents receiving AFDC may end up with less disposable income under this system than if they had relied on Title XX services, and certainly are likely to be able to purchase poorer quality care.

Another federal program supporting child care is the Child Care Food Program. In 1980, 27 million free lunches were served to U.S. children; in 1982 the number dropped to 23 million. Between 1981 and 1984 the program was cut by 30 percent, reducing the funding level from $270 million in 1981 to $130 million in 1984. Child care centers that previously offered two meals and a snack to eligible children may now only offer one meal and no snack. Various forms of programs survive, however, with government assistance, corporate help, or on their own.

Center-Based Programs

In 1977 (the most recent year that figures are available) the National Day Care Study estimated that 18,300 day care centers were in operation. There may be as many as 10,000 more today, and each center has a larger enrollment capacity than those of the past. It is estimated that 50 percent of these centers are nonprofit and the rest are for-profit, some of which belong to "corporate" chains and others are "mom and pop" arrangements that are owner-operated and proprietary. The day care center chains include only 6 percent of all centers (although they claim to serve half the children in licensed care), garnering 9 percent of the revenue. Experts predict that the profit-making chains of centers are likely to grow because they have the start-up capital that small proprietors and not-for-profit entrepreneurs have difficulty raising.

As many as 50 percent of U.S. day care centers may be housed in churches. In 1983 the National Council of Churches of Christ conducted a national study to determine the extent and nature of church-based child care. They estimate that approximately 25,000 day care centers are housed in churches, 14,000 of which are now part of a national church network. Typically, the church serves as a landlord for the center, which uses the space to run its programs. When the church operates the center, it is likely to serve primarily low-income families. The church-based center typically serves fewer than fifty children, and less than a third offer care to infants or school-age children. Religious education is part of the curriculum in a small minority of programs. Approximately 70 percent of the church programs are licensed, although legislation is pending in eight states that would exempt churches from state licensing laws. Child care advocates are generally opposed to these exemptions because they undermine the licensing of all programs. Further, advocates fear the impact on the health, safety, and quality of unregulated church-run programs.

Among an estimated 2,500 employers providing various forms of child care assistance in 1985, 150 corporations sponsor an on- or near-site day care center, and another 400 hospitals and fifty government agencies have created day care centers for their employees. More employers have not started centers because of (1) the high cost of downtown space and start-up; (2) the commuting patterns of employees; (3) the ongoing cost of quality; (4) fears about liability and backlash from employees without children; and (4) the limited number of employees who can benefit from the program.

The employers with centers, however, generally find them worth the effort. Several studies indicate that managers in these companies feel that child care has helped improve recruitment, morale, and productivity. Most employers do not run their centers but rather provide the start-up funds as part of a contract or donation to a community-based organization. An ongoing subsidy may or may not be present. Some experimentation is underway to create revolving loan funds with contributions from employers that would offer a ready supply of needed start-up capital to a variety of groups. Several localities have passed ordinances requiring developers to allot space for child care when constructing new buildings. In San Francisco, the city ordinance requires developers building more than 50,000 square feet of space to include a child care center in the building or to contribute $1 per square foot to a day care fund to be administered by the city. Concord, California, also has this developer requirement in place and several other communities are considering it. A large part of the growth in employer-sponsored child care centers may be attributed to developers, in part because of developer ordinances but also because the "consortium" approach enables the corporate tenants of an industrial park to share the risks, costs, and benefits of establishing a child care program.

Family Day Care

Family day care is the arrangement used by more than 40 percent of preschool children, particularly those under age 3. An estimated 70 percent of these homes are either unlicensed or not required to be licensed. Many family day care providers do not want the intrusion of government regulators, while others are unaware of the advantages of reporting the extra income and claiming deductions for the home-based occupation. Approximately 25 percent of family day care providers are relatives of the children being cared for, and some may not know that they are required by law to be licensed. Several states are trying to put in place a system of registration rather than licensure as a less cumbersome and invasive than traditional licensing in order to encourage these homes to come out from the underground. In general, states with registration systems have experienced massive growth in their coverage of family day care.

These programs are becoming more sophisticated with the advent of family day care networks that provide training, technical assistance, and administrative support to independent providers. The child care food program—which allows family day care providers to receive free food for the children in their care—is often administered through these umbrella agencies. Some individual day care centers take on the coordinating role for family day care by establishing a satellite system of homes that rely on the center for administrative and back-up support.

The growing number and strength of local referral agencies is also helping to stimulate the supply and quality of family day care homes. Companies that contract with local referral agencies want to make sure that care exists, and so funds are provided to hire staff to recruit, train, and monitor new family day care providers. The IBM referral network was directly or indirectly responsible for the creation of 4,500 new family day care homes in the first year of the program's existence (July 1984–85). BankAmerica Foundation also chose family day care as the way to increase the supply of child care. With funds from thirteen California corporations and foundations and six government agencies, BankAmerica spearheaded the Child Care Institute Project. This effort relies on California's statewide referral network to recruit and train new family day care providers. Halfway into the project, in May 1986, the project has helped create more than 100 new family day care homes in the six pilot sites.

Family day care is becoming more attractive to employers as they recognize the unique flexibility that it offers in terms of its (1) *location*, for parents who want their care close to home or work; (2) *ages*, so that both infants and school-age children can be served making one less arrangement for the parent; (3) *hours*, which can accommodate a variety of work shifts; and (4) *expandability*, so that the company can easily absorb a fluctuation in demand.

School-Based Programs

The public school system fills a variety of child care functions. An increasing number of schools offer after-school services, and many already offer care to children ages 3 go 5. In fact, for most 5-year-olds (93 percent) the school is the site of their preschool program (in mandatory kindergartens). Among 3- and 4-year-olds whose mothers work, 43 percent are enrolled in preprimary school programs, a growing number of which are extending the part-time program to cover more of the time that parents work. Centers also develop in schools to serve the children of teenage parents or to educate teenagers about parenting. A variety of community groups may use the school site to run their programs. Some companies, like Wang and those in the Burbank consortium of companies in California, organized a company-sponsored day care center in an empty school building.

These new roles for the school have been adopted because of changing demographics, family lifestyles, and the status of education today. As the debate about school excellence intensifies, the subject of preschool care arises more frequently. Longitudinal research conducted by the High Scope Educational Foundation indicates that quality child care can result in better school readiness, less remedial education, and fewer school drop-outs. With the sound economic arguments behind it, several school districts, such as New York City, are extending the school population downward to include 4-year-olds.

The subject of public school sponsorship of preschool education is not new. In 1974 Albert Shanker advocated public school control of day care in order to find jobs for unemployed teachers. The child care community vigorously debated the merits of this move. The arguments against involvement pertained to the anticipated lack of parent involvement, the use of teachers who were not trained in child development, fears of a curriculum and class size that would be inappropriate for preschoolers, and a system that would not preserve the major strength of the current "system": diversity. As Gwen Morgan of Wheelock College asserts, "Most experts welcome greater school involvement in preschool and day care programs, as long as the school does not become the exclusive delivery system, replacing a diverse system which has value" (Morgan 1986).

Shanker still contends that state legislatures would be more willing to appropriate funds for child care if one institution, such as the schools, would administer the funds. The system could be structured so that the diversity of the current market can be preserved while the disorganization and poor funding can be corrected. Some experts have accepted the inevitability of greater school involvement, and research and policy debates are underway to prepare for that time. Child care experts and school administrators debated the issues at conferences sponsored by Spring Hill in Minneapolis in 1984 and by Yale University's Bush Center in 1986. Bank Street College of Education and Wellesley College are currently examining both state legislation that permits the school to .serve preschoolers and also the experiences of school-supported child care programs currently in place.

Head Start

Begun in 1964, Head Start was the first federal program to acknowledge the importance of the early years. It has become something of a sacred cow (until very recently) and one of the only Great Society programs believed by critics to be effective. In its twenty-year history, Head Start has grown from a $96.4 million program to a $1.1 billion program in 1985. In 1984 about 430,000 children were served—only 20 percent of those eligible (Papageorgiou 1986: 10).

More Head Start programs are becoming full-day in order to serve working parents. (Currently 10 percent are full-day). In addition, about 15 percent of Head Start programs are school-based, although some states have passed legislation that will integrate Head Start into the regular public preschool programs. It is possible that as Head Start evolves (assuming its continued funding) its advocates will join forces with child care advocates. At present, there is little communication between the two factions.

After-School Care

According to the Census Bureau, the numbers of children ages 6 to 11 caring for themselves at home after school is about 2 to 7 million. Institutions are beginning to change to accommodate their needs. Child care centers often take in children after school. More than 1,000 YMCAs and other youth serving agencies, such as Boys Clubs and Girls Scouts, have been providing this service for years. Churches also provide some recreational activity for school-age children in the afternoons. Some profit-making programs exist, such as Kids Clubs, sponsored by KinderCare, the largest commercial chain of day care centers. More than half the independent private schools offer extended day services for their students.

The most obvious institution, the public schools, has only recently focused attention on the needs of their students for after-school care. There are no estimates for the numbers of schools that offer after-school programs, but they have grown considerably in recent years. Many of the school-based programs are school-run; however, many more are run by nonprofit or profit-making community organizations. Some states, such as Tennessee, do not allow school facilities to be used by any group other than a nonprofit association. In Montgomery, Maryland, the school charter allows school space to be used by profit-making organizations, but they are charged more than are nonprofit agencies.

Parents pay between $10 to $25 per week for a program that is typically social and recreational with some informal learning occurring. It is less common for the program to offer a tutoring program, although in many programs the children are assisted with their homework. Transportation is a critical need if the non-school-based programs are to provide safe and reliable alternatives for the after-school care of young children.

Some school systems, however, recognize that a large number of children will be at home alone for several hours after school until their parents return home. Many parents who work on assembly lines or in other jobs cannot be available for telephone calls at 3:15 P.M. In response, a number of community groups around the country have developed "warm lines," or nurturing hotlines, that provide children with a warm and reassuring adult to talk to when they get home from school. Some question the usefulness of these programs and consider them an inadequate although inexpensive alternative for actual care.

Because workers may worry if they have not heard from their children after school or may spend company time talking to them, companies have begun to fund various after-school initiatives. In Houston, a group of thirty-two companies formed the Committee on Private Sector Initiatives to fund eight programs in schools, centers, and storefronts. Chucky Cheese Restaurants are experimenting with an on-site after-school program in their restaurants. KCTV-5 in Kansas City provides the space, publicity, and partial funding for a warm line called Phone Friend. And Phoenix Mutual in Hartford, Connecticut, has offered counseling to parents and their school-age children to determine whether the children were mature enough to stay home alone and if so, to provide them with safety tips.

Sick Child Care

Research out of Portland, Kansas City, and Pennsylvania, indicates that parents may take between eight and twelve days off each year to meet family needs. In addition to possible breakdowns of child care arrangements, a large portion of that time is spent with sick children. To help parents reduce the number of work absences, child care programs, hospitals, community groups, and private companies have developed a variety of programs for the mildly ill child. These include a "get-well" room at a center, a satellite family day care home that cares for sick children, floating staff at a center who can go home and stay with an ill child, and an infirmary specifically for sick children. A number of hospitals have developed in-home nursing services for sick children. These programs cost between $6 and $15 per hour, making them prohibitively expensive when the parent is already paying for the cost of regular child care. 3M Corporation pays 70 percent of the hourly cost of in-home nursing care in order to reduce absenteeism and the financial drain on parents.

In San Jose, California, a fifteen-bed infirmary is attached to a day care center. The Chicken Soup program in Minneapolis is a separately functioning unit with government and business support. Recuperating children can stay at these specially staffed facilities during the day when their parents work. These services reduce, but do not eliminate, the need for parents to be at home some days when their children are sick. Companies can revise their sick leave policies to accommodate parents with seriously ill children. Currently, 26 percent of large corporations offer personal leave that enables parents to stay home with their sick children.

ACCESSIBILITY

The child care system is complex: It is often fragmented, poorly advertised, and varied in quality. A poor choice of care may result in an unhappy child, a frustrated parent, and an inconvenienced employer. In response to the need for consumer information about available child care services more than 200 community-based agencies provide information and referrals to parents seeking care. Many of these programs started within the last decade and evolved out of 4Cs (Community Coordinated Child Care), parent co-ops, and women's organizations. They keep files, increasingly computerized, on the costs, location, hours, curricula, and availability of child care programs. The resource and referral agencies (R&R's) also provide counseling to parents to help them understand the system and determine their optimal form of care. They are then given several referrals to investigate, often accompanied by a checklist of what constitutes quality and how to identify it. R&R's do not make recommendations in order to enhance the parent's consumer responsibility and protect themselves from liability. The referral agency does not refer parents to care that operates outside the law.

These services are typically funded by a patchwork of sources that may include local government, United Way, and employer contracts. Sometimes a fee is charged to the general public, but the service is often provided free of charge to local residents. California is the first state with a statewide network of resource and referral agencies. Its network was begun in 1974 with $9 million of state funds and now includes over sixty referral agencies. Other states are now considering legislation that would establish similar statewide referral systems. Those that have begun to fund a referral system include Massachusetts, New Jersey, North Carolina, New Mexico, and Florida. Policymakers have recognized the importance of R&R for matching the supply and demand of services, collecting data on the unmet need, recruiting new services, and providing training and technical assistance to providers to improve service quality.

R&R's also provide a convenient first step for employers who do not want to start new child care programs but who want to assess the level and direction of need among their employees. Approximately 500 employers contract with local R&R's to provide their employees with counseling and referral services and to make reports back to the company about the scope of need among employees. Some also provide on-site counseling and parent education seminars. When an R&R does not exist in the community, the company may start an in-house program. In Minneapolis, Hartford, Connecticut, and Holland, Minnesota, a consortium of companies created a new I&R agency.

The sophistication of the R&R contract was greatly advanced when IBM established nationwide service in 200 plant sites. The company contracted with Work/Family Directions, a Boston-based firm, to identify local agencies that IBM employees can call for counseling, consumer education, and referral. This local agency recruits new providers and assists them in start-up. Additional funds are provided to local agencies to offer training to improve the quality of the supply of child care services. Within one year of program operation, IBM support to Work/Family Directions was directly or indirectly responsible for creating over 5,000 new child care programs, most of which were provided in family day care homes.

Through employer contracts referral programs can help parents become wise consumers. Most company contract programs provide literature that helps parents identify and evaluate quality in the programs they visit. Some local R&R contractors report, however, that parent expectations can be raised to unrealistic levels, unable to find or afford the quality recommended by the experts.

AFFORDABILITY

For working families, child care is the fourth largest budget item—exceeded only by food, housing, and taxes. Child care costs typically absorb 10 percent of a family's budget; for a family with two preschoolers, child care can amount to as much as 30 percent of household income.

The costs of child care vary according to the numbers and ages of children needing care, the type of care chosen, and the number of hours care is used. All of these factors are related to the income and education levels of the parents. One study suggests that 64 percent of all 3- and 4-year olds living in families with incomes greater than $20,000 are enrolled in some form of child care outside the child's home. Families with incomes below $20,000 are more likely to rely on relatives or family day care arrangements, which are usually less expensive (Kamerman 1982: 8).

Care for infants and toddlers (children under age 3) tends to be more expensive than care for preschoolers. Center-based care is typically more expensive than care for a preschooler in a family day care home. The least expensive programs are those serving school-age children because they are used for fewer hours during the day. An in-home caregiver, unrelated to the child, is the most expensive form of care. The minimum wage law applies if the caregiver works twenty hours a week. At $250 per week, child care would cost $13,000 per year, plus Social Security, unemployment, and worker's compensation, which increase the cost by 10 percent.

There are also significant regional differences in the costs of care for children of various ages and for each type of care. Much of this difference can be attributed to state licensing standards. For instance, it is most expensive to purchase child care in the Northeast, where standards are high, and it is cheapest in the South, where standards are lower. Because of these variations in quality, out-of-home care for one child can cost anywhere from $1,500 to $10,000 per year, with the majority of parents paying $3,000 per year for child care services.

According to *Forbes* magazine in 1982, the need for child care creates an estimated $10 billion a year service industry (Byrne and Brown 1982: 203). Parents pay approximately 70 percent of the costs of running these programs. Sliding fee scales can help lower-income families afford program fees, but only a minority of programs vary their fees by income.

In recognition of child care as a work-related expense, the federal government created the Dependent Care Tax Credit in 1976. In 1982 over 5 million families received $1.5 billion in child care credits. In 1983 child care credits increased to $2.06 billion. As amended in 1982 a 30 percent credit may be taken by families with adjusted gross incomes of $10,000 or less; the credit is reduced by 1 percent for each $2,000 increase in income and is limited to a 20 percent credit for those with incomes of $30,000 or more. The credit ranges from $480 to $720 for one child and from $960 to $1,440 for two or more children.

The credit may not be claimed against expenses in excess of $2,400 for one child and $4,800 for two children, but as indicated earlier, average costs exceed these amounts. In addition, the credit cannot be greater than the filer's tax liability. As a result, many low-income families cannot take advantage of the credit, although some contend that these families should get direct subsidies rather than rely on the tax system. Only 15 percent of families using the credit in 1982 had incomes below $12,000. Two-thirds of the credits went to those earning $20,000 or more. Efforts to require refundability—enabling those whose tax liability is less than the amount of the credit they deserve to receive a refund—have failed. President Reagan has proposed that there be a $60,000 cap on the income levels of those who can apply for the child care credit. This provision is not part of the current tax reform initiatives.

Another strategy for making child care more affordable is embodied in section 129 of the 1981 Economic Recovery Tax Act (ERTA), which authorized the creation of Dependent Care Assistance Plans (DCAPs). This provision made child care a nontaxable benefit for the employee and a tax-deductible contribution for the employer. Legislators anticipated that this provision would motivate employers to create voucher plans under which employers subsidize a portion of employees' child care costs. However, as a nontaxable benefit, child care became a convenient addition to flexible benefit plans. Most of these plans involve a program of salary reduction but no employer contribution. Rather, in this type of plan, employees reduce their taxable income and use pretax dollars to pay for their dependents' care. As a result, a dependent care option in flexible benefits is the most prevalent form of child care assistance, currently provided by an estimated 1,000 employers. Of concern is the fact that families whose incomes are below $26,000 may fare better under the Dependent Care Tax Credit than they would under salary reduction.

Other employers provide financial assistance through discounts and, on a very limited basis, vouchers. Approximately 300 employers have negotiated reduced rates for their employees at local child care centers. Most programs, usually those in profit-making chains, offer a 10 percent discount to the employees, and in about half the contracts, the employer contributes 10 percent of the fees so that employees benefit from a 20 percent reduction in their child care costs.

In a voucher program employers reimburse employees for a portion of the costs incurred at a child care program selected by the parent. Only about twenty-five companies offer vouchers because of their potential expense and the existence of the less expensive alternative in flexible benefits with salary reduction. At the Ford Foundation and Polaroid Corporation, the voucher is available only to those employees whose family incomes are less than $30,000 in order to help those in greatest need.

QUALITY

The research on program quality is clear: We know and can control the determinants of quality. Research indicates that group size and caregiver qualifications have the greatest influence on quality. Staff-child ratios are also important, as are the goals, educational philosophy, and curriculum, but these are only as effective as the people hired to implement them. Yet training monies have been cut out of federal programs and are difficult to find elsewhere. More than 10,000 caregivers have received the Child Development Associate degree, a competency-based training program administered by the National Association for the Education of Young Children (NAEYC).

This federally funded program has also been cut. Those with proper training often question their future in child care. The work is demanding, and it offers low pay and few benefits. Child care workers are now subjected to fingerprinting for criminal background checks to reduce the potential of sexual abuse. These working conditions have led to a nationwide shortage of child care staff. An additional drain on the supply of workers is the competition from the increasing number of school-based programs that offer higher wages and union protection.

In Title XX centers, day care staff wages place them at two-thirds of the poverty level. Over 85 percent of family day care providers make below the minimum wage, and 94 percent of wages are below the poverty level. A Massachusetts study found that day care workers earn $6.40 per day, while kennel workers' fees are $8 per day. Approximately 63 percent of the state's child care workers had no health coverage. A study of 95 child care workers in thirty-two New York City day care centers found that staff were in the lower 10 percent of adult earners in the city, despite the fact that 70 percent of them had college degrees or graduate degrees. More than half had no medical coverage as part of their employment.

The state regulatory systems need revision: Some states have silly, onerous requirements, while others have provisions that cannot protect the health and safety of young children. Furthermore, many states have permitted their staffing commitment to erode to the point where they are not adequately inspecting child care centers and family day care homes.

The accreditation program begun by the National Association for the Education of Young Children may encourage providers to strive for higher quality and to help the public understand that there are levels of quality higher than the minimum permitted by licensing. It is also possible that the efforts of AT&T to research and invest in the quality of child care will offset the damage that has been done with the decline of standards.

One issue that undercuts the reputation of child care is the recent insurance crisis in child care. It is assumed by many that child care programs are not good insurance risks because of the likelihood of abuse and accidents. The negative publicity about sexual abuse scandals came at a time when the insurance industry was facing a crisis. Like municipal police departments, midwives, and ski resorts, child care programs have had their premiums skyrocket or canceled entirely. According to a 1985 survey by the *Child Care Information Exchange* and the Child Care Action Campaign, 20 percent of child care programs have had their insurance policies canceled, and 30 percent have had their rates increase over 100 percent. An increase of 300 percent is not uncommon.

As Deborah Phillips of NAEYC testified in congressional hearings on the subject, "The loss of insurance and prohibitive rate increases . . . bear no relation to the professionalism, quality or claims history of the programs affected." For instance, a program in Indiana with excellent staff-to-child ratios and directed by a registered nurse had its annual premium raised from $3,200 to $9,000. The program had never filed a claim but would need to charge parents an additional $144 per year to cover increased insurance costs. Unable to pass these costs along to parents, child care programs are sacrificing quality in order to pay insurance premiums. It is hoped that the agreement forged between Continental Insurance and a coalition of national organizations will mitigate the hardships caused by the insurance problem.

While some advocate for better wages and work conditions, other child care groups focus on increasing the level of professionalism in the field. The goals of higher wages and increased prestige require that the cost of child care be increased. Because 80 percent of a child care center's budget is staff, programs cannot absorb the cost of wage increases for staff. Parents are also unable to withstand increased fees. Companies seem unwilling to subsidize the costs, and government is abandoning its commitment. The present system has the staff paying a high cost in accepting wages too low for their qualifications and the value of their work. In certain states, children pay the cost by spending time in poor-quality care. Who will pay for the high-quality child care that we hear parents demand but that they cannot afford? Can society afford *not* to provide high-quality care to generations of young children? If not, how will children's later schooling and their productivity as the labor force of the future be affected by low-quality child care?

WHO IS RESPONSIBLE FOR PROVIDING CHILD CARE?

Child care services today are largely a grassroots phenomenon that has flourished in response to a community need. That is, in part, why services have grown topsy-turvy. Government and corporations are two potential benefactors of the child care system that are described below in terms of their willingness to offer support. It is important to note that other supporters of the system, such as United Way, civic groups, and parents must also contribute if there is ever to be an adequate system of child care.

Government Support

Government support for child care has focused largely on: (a) broad policy objectives such as reducing welfare dependency, improving the economy, or aiding in some national emergency such as war when companies need women to help in the war effort; or (b) narrower objectives such as protection and treatment for deprived, abused, or neglected children. While laudable goals, they are not solely child focused, and the funding streams often reflect it.

The patchwork of funding for child care persists despite five attempts to pass comprehensive child care legislation that would address the availability, affordability, accessibility, and quality of the system. The first attempt was called the Comprehensive Child Development Act of 1971. This bill was overwhelmingly passed by both houses of Congress but became the victim of the infamous Nixon veto in which he likened child care to the "Soviet style" of raising children. The bill was reintroduced in 1972 but then did not pass the Congress. Efforts in 1974 and 1975 were made by then-Senator Mondale and Representative Brademas. Their Child and Family Services Act never reached the floor for a vote. A similar fate was met by the last two efforts to secure adequate funding for child care— one introduced by Senator Cranston in 1979 and the other by Representative Miller in 1984 as the Omnibus Child Care Act.

The bills failed because of a host of moral and political issues that in and of themselves have nothing to do with the merits of child care support. Nixon was interested in passing his family assistance plan that was to include child care support. The Moral Majority organized a mail campaign against the Child and Family Services Act charging that child care proponents were seeking to destroy the American family. In the 1980s, during a period of recessions, deficits, and military build-ups, child care funding has not seen supported by members of Congress or the administration.

While program monies have not been forthcoming, subsidies to middle-income parents through the Dependent Care Tax Credit have doubled since 1980. And there has been considerable effort to encourage the private sector to support what government has been less willing or able to fund. A special Subcommittee on Child Care was established in 1982 as part of President Reagan's Task Force on Private Sector Initiatives. Thirty-four breakfasts were held for company presidents to learn about the need for child care and possible business solutions. This effort helped educate corporate decision-makers and lent credibility to the issue because of White House sponsorship. Questions remain, however, about the overall effectiveness of this strategy, given limited efforts on the part of government to improve the child care system that would facilitate employer involvement and help those in greatest need.

Employer Support

Employer interest in child care began during the Civil War when manufacturers of ammunition and soldiers' clothing needed women to help in the war effort. For the same reasons, hospitals and other industries offered on-site day care centers during World War I and, with government assistance, during World War II. Industry's interest in child care remained dormant until the late 1960s, when company interest in child care reflected the trend toward corporate social responsibility. But it was not until a decade later that child care became a legitimate business issue that was capable of affecting the bottom-line.

In 1979 an estimated 115 companies and hospitals provided child care, mostly in the form of on-site day care centers. By 1981 the number had jumped to 600, and their responses were focused on referral services and flexible benefits. According to The Conference Board, there were, in 1985, 2,500 employers providing some form of child care support. This growth is largely attributable to a sudden recognition of the change in workforce demographics, a change caused largely by the labor force participation of mothers with young children. Outside pressure mounted as service providers began marketing their services to business in the hopes of recouping what government seemed less willing or able to fund. And public/private partnerships became a popular concept promoted by a popular president. A generally favorable business climate and tax changes have provided greater opportunities for corporate involvement. Because growth industries—such as the high technology industry, banks, insurance companies, and hospitals—have the capital to invest, they have become the pioneers of child care.

The specific form of an employer's response to child care will depend on a unique blend of (1) management objectives (the company's expected return on investment), (2) parent needs (the specific child care problems of that workforce), and (3) community resources (where are the gaps in services that frustrate employees?). As a result, child care solutions are tailored to each company, and no two companies have implemented precisely the same type of program. In addition, the prevalence of employer support is uneven.

One may find employer support where there are concentrations of high-growth industries, such as Research Triangle, North Carolina, and Route 128 near Boston. One will also find corporate involvement where there is a sophisticated child care community. The direction of current employer involvement indicates that business is more interested in helping their employees buy into the existing system of child care than in creating new services. They accomplish this by helping them find child care through information and referral services or by helping them pay for child care through discounts, vouchers, and flexible benefits.

While the growth of employer involvement has been dramatic, there are still more than 6 million employers who have not responded. Though relatively limited, employer-supported child care is having a positive effect on the child care system. If nothing else, corporate scrutiny of the child care system has revealed major gaps in services. Internal work policies have also had an effect on the child care system. For instance, alternative work schedules may solve some of the conflict between work and family life. However, flextime requires that child care programs adapt to new schedules, which by their very purpose will vary from family to family. And part-time work options, such as job sharing and work-at-home programs, raise similar questions about how child care providers are to charge fees or organize a curriculum and staffing pattern with different children present at various times of the day and week.

Employers cannot meet the need for child care alone. In fact, no one sector can infuse the dollars into the system that will secure enough high-quality care that parents can afford. At a minimum, government must address those in greatest need: the unemployed, those looking for work, and those in job training. Government also has a responsibility to the vast majority of parents who work in small companies that cannot provide child care benefits and services. A stronger federal and state commitment to creating an adequate system of child care for working parents would strengthen the field and ultimately facilitate employer involvement. Most critical to the encouragement of private sector support is the development of an infrastructure that businesses can invest in. We saw from the pattern of corporate support that it tends to build on what is already available in the community. If the community is limited, then so are the opportunities for company participation. Child care is clearly an area ripe for public/private partnerships.

The massive funding that the system requires will not be forthcoming in the near future. Economic explanations can be offered for this, but ideological barriers are just as difficult to overcome. Day care is generally misunderstood, in part because little data have been collected about its use. It is also misperceived as a woman's issue, when in fact it is a family issue, and as a social issue, rather than as an economic issue. It is too often thought of as a custodial babysitting service for the poor. Given the extent of child care use across income categories, it should be considered a public utility. Child care is not central to anyone's agenda, in concept or funding. It is misrepresented in that women's groups, government, and the business community do not actively advocate for increased child care support, despite the fact that it serves their self-interests.

In spite of the obstacles, occasional innovations energize proponents of child care. And some problems can be blessings in disguise. While the system is disorganized and fragmented, it is also diverse and capable of offering parents a range of program choices. As long as caregiver wages remain low, parents are better able to afford care. In addition to considerable increases in funding, the child care field needs a public relations campaign. Somehow, the image of child care must be improved before the future picture of child care can reflect a commitment to children and families and the support from many sectors of society.

REFERENCES

Byrne, John A., and Paul B. Brown. 1982. "Those Unpredictable Babies." *Forbes* (November 22): 203–208.

Kamerman, Sheila B. 1983. "Child Care Services: A National Picture." *Monthly Labor Review* (December): 35–39.

_____. "Child Care Services: A National Picture." Paper presented at The MacArthur Foundation Conference on *Child Care: Growth-Fostering Environments For Young Children*, Chicago, Illinois, November 29–December 1, 1982.

Morgan, Gwen. Interview. Boston, Massachusetts, May 15, 1986.

Papageorgiou, Mary. 1986. *The National Preschool Data Base.* Position Paper. Washington, D.C.: Center for Statistics, January.

U.S. Bureau of Labor Statistics. 1983.

U.S. Bureau of the Census. 1982. *Current Population Reports.* Washington, D.C.: U.S. Government Printing Office.

_____. 1982. *Current Population Survey.* Washington, D.C.: U.S. Government Printing Office.

_____. 1984. *Current Population Reports.* Washington, D.C.: U.S. Government Printing Office.

9 EARLY CHILDHOOD EDUCATION AND THE PUBLIC SCHOOLS

Albert Shanker

In a recent op-ed piece in the *New York Times*, Kenneth Woodward and Arthur Kornhaber (1985), authors of *Grandparents/Grandchildren: The Vital Connection*, argue that young people today, in matters of emotional development, mature later than ever before. "To become adults," they say, "the young need to be around adults." With the fragmentation of families we are increasingly a society "profoundly segregated by age." Children, day in and day out, are exposed to fewer and fewer models of grownup behavior. All this, of course, as they point out, has profound implications for education—for our methods, for our expectations.

It is also another good case for returning to the old-fashioned extended family—mom and dad, grandma and grandpa, Uncle Joe and Aunt Suzy, all living down the block or around the corner from each other. But it is highly unlikely that the good old days will be back. All signs point to a continuing erosion of family life. The divorce rate has not abated, and single-parent households grow in number. Almost one-fifth of all births in 1980 were to unmarried women. In addition, the percentage of working mothers with children under age 18 increased from 18 percent in 1948 to the current rate of 54 percent. It is now also estimated that about 40 percent of the children between ages 3 and 5 have mothers in the workforce. Furthermore, millions of disadvantaged children have parents who, though at home, lack the resources to provide an adequate home environment, and these conditions are likely to continue. As a result, more and more children are being raised a large part of the time by someone outside the family. Currently 6.2 million youngsters are in some sort of preschool program, and it is estimated that this number will increase by a million in the next decade (Greene 1985: 4). As one commentator put it recently (Bronfenbrenner 1985: 8), as far as the family is concerned, "Caring [for children] is becoming a lost art." Clearly, whether we like it or not, the need to provide adequate day care for millions of children will remain an urgent national priority.

All this is happening at a time when there is mounting evidence that the preschool years are crucial in a child's emotional and intellectual development. Within the last thirty years, the works of educators like Benjamin Bloom and Jean Piaget have supported the idea that the young child should be deliberately exposed to stimulating experiences rather than simply left on his own. A new study of 175 disadvantaged children done by the University of North Carolina at Chapel Hill concluded that good preschools can raise IQs by as much as fifteen points and significantly improve later grade-school achievement ("Children Who Attend" 1985: 6). The recent landmark longitudinal study of the Ypsilanti Perry Preschool project convincingly documents the economic and intellectual gains and the benefits to society accruing from a well-planned preschool program (*Changed Lives* 1984).

The key is quality. Many experts have warned about the detrimental effects of substandard day care. Mere custodial care, even in well-maintained facilities, does not provide the child with the ingredients necessary for the development of sound learning skill and a healthy personality. Many psychologists and psychiatrists have misgivings about the emotional impact of early childhood education programs in general and warn, as one writer put it (Boyd 1976: 28), "that anything but quality day care is clearly damaging to a child."

As a nation we are faced with the opportunity to meet a growing demand for a service that at its best is manifestly beneficial. Regardless of what we do about that opportunity, more and more young children will be placed in some sort of day care facility. Parents will, of necessity, settle for mere custodial care if none other is offered. Our goal should be to make high-quality preschool universally avail-

able as it is in France where the *Ecole maternelle* provides for 88 percent of the nation's 3-year-olds and all 4-year-olds (Bennett 1985:
4). This schooling cannot be provided through our present fragmented delivery system.

We can provide ready access and consistently high standards only
by making the public schools the primary sponsors of such programs.
The first advantage of such a proposal is that schools already are
available throughout the country in urban, suburban, small town,
and rural areas. Moreover, communities that have experienced declines in school enrollment can make more efficient use of existing
plants by adding preschool classes to their existing programs. The
ultimate aim is to give parents the same option of utilizing a highly
desirable service that they now have for kindergarten. We also can
begin to diminish the inequities we see developing where attendance
in high-quality programs increasingly depends on the size of a family's income. Our current course might well create a two- or three-
tier system that reinforces prevailing societal inequalities.

A second asset of public school systems is that they already have
in place organizations experienced and adept in administering large
and complicated federal projects. They can quickly implement new
programs without the cost and effort of establishing a new bureau-
cracy. Within this organizational structure, enormously difficult
questions remain to be addressed. For example, to what extent shall
the school day for young children be extended to accommodate parents' work schedules? What role, if any, would private providers have
in a publicly sponsored system? Should home care or extended
maternity leaves be encouraged in place of more formal day care,
as many experts advocate? What should be done about the fastest
growing group of youngsters—children under age 1 with working
mothers? It is unlikely that satisfactory answers to these questions
can be provided by our current hit-or-miss approach. Letting a million blossoms bloom may be good poetry, but in this case it is hardly
a substitute for sound, unified social policy. One community institution should be designated to coordinate efforts to deal with these
and other related problems. Our schools are in the best position to
carry out this mission.

Third, our schools are better equipped than isolated day care centers to offer and effectively coordinate the varied diagnostic, counseling, and health services needed by young children. For example, eye

examinations and hearing tests, now routinely done by many schools, could be provided for children earlier if early childhood programs were part of the public school system. Also, if a child's physical, emotional or intellectual readiness for a particular program were in doubt, a public school, not guided by the profit motive, would likely be willing and able to provide competent screening procedures to guide parents. Many school districts, including Ossining, New York, now require candidates for kindergarten and first grade to be tested to determine if they are ready for school. In Los Angeles, for instance, 146 public schools already offer a voluntary school-readiness program. These districts would undoubtedly extend the same services to preschoolers under their care, which refutes those who claim that linking early childhood education and the public schools will thrust all children into a premature and potentially damaging exposure to academic subjects. Finally, the diagnostic and testing resources of the public schools would put us in a better position to monitor exactly what is going on in our early childhood classrooms. Extensive, centralized testing and supervision would provide both the information we need to refine our curriculums and also the methodology to help us determine if resources are being used effectively.

Most important, using our public school systems could solve the problem of staffing that has severely undercut confidence in our present day care industry. Reports from across the country indicate that in many cases insurance companies are doubling or tripling the liability premiums for day care centers. Sometimes they have simply canceled policies, forcing some operators to close up shop. All this is a result of adverse publicity generated by a number of child-abuse cases: Seven indictments were handed down in California as a result of the alleged abuse of 100 children over a number of years; the entire staff of an Alabama center was dismissed on similar charges; in New York City, six day care employees were arrested for allegedly abusing thirty-nine children.

It is unfair to condemn a whole group for the misdeeds of a relative few, but these latest scandals are simply extreme manifestations of a problem identified more than a decade ago by reports like *Windows on Day Care* (Keyserling 1972) and *Early Schooling in the United States* (1973), which documented the poor conditions found in many day care establishments and the inadequate professional training received by most staffs. According to federal figures for 1983, twenty-one states had no minimum requirements for day care teachers, and twenty-six others required only a high school diploma. At a 1984 congressional hearing, Representative Beryl Anthony, Jr., of Arkansas pointed out that "only about 25 percent of the employees of child care operations around the country have had professional training in dealing with children." [1]

About the same time, *Newsweek* ("What Price Day Care?" 1984: 19) offered a summary of the inherent problems of staffing private day care centers: "At the big centers, most workers receive the minimum wage of $3.35 an hour. . . . In theory, state licensing bodies ought to be able to screen out the sexual molesters, at least those with prior convictions. In practice, most licensing requirements are lax, and state agencies don't have the money or the manpower to regulate the day-care industry at all rigorously." Congress was sufficiently concerned about the problem to earmark $25 million in 1984 for a one-year state grant program to set up machinery to check the background of all employees of day care facilities. Once again, however, it is up to the state, if it chooses to participate, to establish its own investigative guidelines. Based on the record, the outlook for stringent standards is hardly promising.

In contrast, most public school systems have in place a tried system of testing candidates for teaching positions and authenticating their credentials as well as a system of supervision and evaluation to identify and weed out incompetents. Though salary scales are generally far below professional standards, schools have long traditions of acceptable staff behavior that help establish at least some restraint on the very few problem teachers who slip through the screening process.

The history of Head Start, probably the most widely publicized early childhood project, offers another powerful argument for putting all such programs under the jurisdiction of the public schools. Dr. Robert E. Cooke, a pediatrician who served as chairman of the original Head Start planning committee, was quoted recently as saying that Head Start was "the most successful social experiment of the 20th century" (Bridgman 1985: 22). Certainly the results of the program are impressive, and many of us share Cooke's enthusiam. In spite of the "success" he claims that Head Start has enjoyed through a series of administrations, however, the program still reaches only approximately 19 percent of the income eligible children. The Reagan administration proposes to freeze the current level of expenditure for fiscal 1986, which means that given even modest inflation it is likely that the number of children serviced will decline.

A graph showing participation in Head Start since 1965 illustrates the vicissitudes of even the best of programs. It has had what another member of the original planning committee calls a "Perils of Pauline existence" (Bridgman 1985: 21), and at several points it was almost phased out despite its success. Ups and downs are inevitable for any program based on a relatively narrow constituency. As long as programs are viewed as frills or exclusively antipoverty projects, they never will be fully funded and will suffer from the shifts of administration ideologies and the constraints of budgets.

Through good times and bad, support for public schools as reflected in referenda and local budgets has remained relatively constant. During economic downturns, teachers may not get salary increases that they deserve or class sizes might increase, but no one seriously advocates doing away with the second grade or cutting out the last year of high school. It is taken for granted that the integrity of the total school program must be maintained for the good of the children. In the same way, early childhood education should become one of the givens of the public school system and not be subject to the whims of fashion or partisanship or the fluctuations of the economy. Only when such programs are under the protection of the broad constituency of the public schools can such a fundamental change of consciousness be brought about.

Many critics will be quick to point out that the recent record of our public schools does not inspire much confidence that they can successfully take on any new responsibility. Report after report has documented the allegedly dismal performance of our students. This bad press is not surprising, since our public schools are on the front line and bear the burden of all well-publicized social problems. But the total balance sheet shows that there are also many fine things going on in our classrooms—innovative, effective teaching, prize-winning student projects, and first-rate preparation for our best colleges. The truth is that the faults are known and widely reported only because public schools are fully accountable to local taxpayers and elected officials: We do not know much about what is going on in the private education sector. This is particularly true of our patchwork delivery system for early childhood education. The shift that I advocate means turning away from private organizations that are not subject to democratic policymaking and that are geared largely to securing high profit margins. By contrast, public schools are consistently among the most responsive and sensitive government institutions.

This responsiveness and sensitivity are important in another context. Even a casual examination of a large school system—like New York City's, for example—will show that our administrators and teachers are extremely flexible and open to new approaches. One can list one exciting, innovative program after another—the City as School, released time for elementary school students for ballet lessons or for work on science projects with university professors, artists in residence conducting studio classes, farming and animal husbandry within the city limits, and much more. The point is that commitment to public school control of early childhood education is not a commitment to uniformity or rigidity. School systems would be free to expand and vary their services to meet local needs or even certify and fund private organizations that were providing high-quality service. In this way flexibility would be coupled with better coordination of effort and superior quality control.

Perhaps the most formidable argument against implementing a universal early childhood public school program is, as usual, the cost. A sympathetic observer recently estimated that the bill for only half the children between ages 3 and 5 would come to a prohibitive $25 billion. We are certainly not likely to get anything approaching this sum from the combined federal, state, and local governments, particularly in a time of deficit and retrenchment. But this is all the more reason to try new perspectives and reassess our current practices. For example, what I have been proposing does not have to be an "add-on" to existing systems. We might adopt New York State Commissioner of Education Gordon Ambach's proposal that students start their schooling at age 4 and finish high school at 17. We might also reorganize the way we utilize our teachers, perhaps by making more use of videotapes where they would be more effective than lectures. We might get college or high school students into our lower-grade and early childhood classrooms to serve as tutors or counselors. In other words, an imaginative restructuring of our present system could improve education and at the same time significantly cut into the cost of implementing a preschool program.

Another way to look at the question of cost is to realize that it is not a matter of whether or not to spend the money but of *when* to spend it. Society bears the burden of the enormous expense of juvenile crime, teenage pregnancy, drug use, and school dropouts. We have tried the costly approach of solving our problems rather than preventing them, but recent studies have made clear that an investment in high-quality early childhood education with high-risk children pays off later in significantly reduced social problems and in greater academic and economic achievement. We can pay now to promote a higher quality of life or later to try to mitigate the fruits of our neglect. As David Weikart (1984: 25), president of the High/Scope Educational Research Foundation, put it recently, "It is cheaper to provide early education as prevention than to pay for more costly social remediation later on." The bottom line is that early intervention is a good deal for the taxpayer.

It is difficult for Americans to face the unpleasant truth that we really do not serve our children as well as we might. The figures for teenage pregnancy, drunken driving, suicide, and school dropouts paint a picture of widespread drift and neglect. The most recent statistics on poverty show that the fastest-growing group of poor people in our country are children under age 5. Surely we must do better. Fortunately, what we now know about the value of early childhood education points to what we might do for the next generation to avoid the blunders of the past and the waste of so many of our young people. As quickly as possible we must go beyond experimental projects to a full-scale, nationwide commitment. Our public schools are the nearest instruments at hand for the swiftest, most effective implementation of this vital policy.

NOTES

1. See report of U.S. House Select Committee on Children, Youth, and Families (1984: 9, 113). At the same hearing Representative Mario Biaggi (Dem. N.Y.) reiterated Anthony's point (U.S. House Select Committee 1984: 12).

REFERENCES

Bennet, Andrew. 1985. "Partnership and Choice." *London Times* (February 1): 4.

Boyd, Marjorie. 1976. "The Case against Day Care." *Washington Monthly* 8 (December): 28.

Bridgman, Anne. 1985. "Head Start at 20." *Education Week* (May 8): 22.

Bronfenbrenner, Urie. 1985. "The Three Worlds of Childhood." *Principal* 6, no. 5 (May): 8.

Changed Lives. 1984. Monographs of the High/Scope Educational Research Foundation. Ypsilanti, Michigan.

"Children Who Attend Top-Quality Preschools." 1985. *USA Today* (March 13): 6.

Goodlad, John, et al. 1983. *Early Schooling in the United States.* New York: McGraw-Hill.

Greene, Leon. 1985. "As the Twig Is Bent." *Principal* 6 (May): 4.

Keyserling, Mary. 1972. *Windows on Day Care.* New York: National Council of Jewish Women.

U.S. House Select Committee on Children, Youth, and Families. 1984. Hearing on *Families and Child Care: Improving the Options.* 98th Cong., 2nd Sess. Serial 98-109. September 17, 1984.

Weikart, David. 1984. "Changed Lives." *American Education* 21 (Winter): 25.

"What Price Day Care?" 1984. *Newsweek* (September 10): 14-18.

Woodward, Kenneth L., and Arthur Kornhaber. 1985. "Youth Is Maturing Later." *New York Times.* May 10.

_____ 1981. *Grandparents/Grandchildren: The Vital Connection.* Garden City, N.Y.: Doubleday.

10 THE ETHICS OF A PUBLIC PRESCHOOL

Jerome Kagan

A tension in our society between two almost incompatible desires is forcing many citizens to make an ethical decision regarding the care of young children. On the one hand, a large number of citizens agree on the need for quality surrogate care for young children of working mothers. The situation is especially serious for economically disadvantaged families. The quality of surrogate care for these children is not as benevolent as it should be, but the cost of better care is beyond the economic resources of the average working-class parent. For these reasons, there are obvious advantages to legislation that will create mandatory public school for ages 2 through 5 supported by public funds.

Although such an action would have benevolent consequences for some parents, it would be inconsistent with the desires of an equally large number of middle-class mothers who choose not to work, many of whom have psychologically gratifying relationships with their young children. As a result, both mother and child are benefiting from their time together at home. It is not clear that requiring these 3-year-old children to attend school will be psychologically beneficial. The conflict, therefore, is between the practical needs of a large number of families whose children may be at potential risk and freedom of choice for an equally large number of children whose development seems more sanguine.

101

In such conflict situations one always tries to find some rational, and hopefully factual, basis for action that might resolve the dilemma. It is likely that those who will make the decision will use pragmatic criteria, and the child's future adjustment to U.S. society is likely to be the dimension chosen to guide the decision process. I do not favor voluntary school attendance because our society would end up with a two-class structure in which the less-advantaged mothers who must work will put their children in school and many middle-class mothers who do not work will keep their children at home. Mandatory busing in the 1970s led to the creation of many private schools because parents did not want their children in the same environment with minority children. Such a situation is inimical to the egalitarian ethic we value. For that reason a voluntary system is potentially dangerous.

The pragmatic question most will ask is simply whether mandatory preschool will increase the probability that more Americans will obtain better jobs, firmer economic security, and a greater sense of dignity if all children attend school during the first five years. However, it is not obvious that these goals will be the sequelae of early schooling because the major determinant of a good job is not now, and has never been, how much knowledge an individual child or adult possesses in the absolute sense. In industrialized societies each child and adolescent holds a rank in relation to other children with respect to his or her academic ability. It is the child's relative rank that determines the quality of college attended and the status or quality of the vocation eventually attained. The average child in a disadvantaged area of Boston in 1985 has more knowledge than a middle-class child of a physician who lived in rural New Hampshire a century ago. But the former child is in the bottom 10 percent of New England children, and the latter was probably in the top 10 percent of his reference group. Harvard undergraduates in 1985 read, write, and spell less proficiently than Harvard undergraduates did in 1965. Yet the same top 10 percent of graduating seniors are admitted to our best schools of medicine, law, and architecture, and I suggest that the quality of medicine, law, and architecture has not deteriorated over the past twenty years.

Most parents see intellectual growth and academic progress as a ladder with a delineated top that they believe all children can attain. The corollary belief is that all those who approach the top are guaranteed a successful life. However, a more apt metaphor for intellectual and academic development is a racetrack. The winner is not determined by the speed of an individual horse but rather by a particular horse's speed in relation to the other horses in the race. Recognition of that fact informs our earlier question of whether a majority of children will benefit from mandatory preschool.

I suspect that about 2 million of the approximately 10 million U.S. children between ages 2 and 5 will be helped by mandatory preschool attendance. Many come from economically disadvantaged homes. These children will probably be more advanced in their knowledge of letters and numbers when they reach first grade if they have attended school than if they had been in surrogate care. Thus, the relative rank of these children will probably be raised by school attendance. But there is an equal number of children from middle-class homes who may not benefit. Some may fall in the rank order, especially those children with nonworking mothers who have psychologically good relationships with their parents. Many of these children will be better prepared for the first grade if they remain at home than if they go to school. For the majority of the remaining 6 million children it will probably not make much difference which regimen of care they experience. If these rough estimates are correct, then we have an ethical dilemma. We must decide which group of children is to be the primary beneficiary—the first or the second.

Resolution of this issue is not to be decided by science alone with objective facts dictating the ethically correct decision. My personal philosophy is that contemporary historical conditions should be an important determinant of the beneficiary chosen in a situation of moral conflict. If we were living in New York when it was called New Amsterdam, most citizens would not side with the economically disadvantaged family. But because contemporary society has become more interdependent and egalitarian than it was in the early eighteenth century, it is ethically more defensible to choose the health of the larger society as the primary beneficiary of a political action. Because I believe the larger society will benefit from mandatory public school for young children, I favor that decision. But I might not prefer it a century from now and probably would not have voted for it a hundred years earlier.

There are, however, some facts that make this ethical decision a bit less sentimental and slightly more rational. One reason for mandatory preschool derives from the fact that the primary cause of delinquency, which costs this nation many millions of dollars annually, is academic failure, especially reading failure, in elementary school. The best predictor of delinquency in adolescence, after social class is controlled, is reading failure in the second or third grades. If more children were prepared for the task of reading by their entrance into grade one, we would prevent more academic failures. Another major advantage of preschool is the possibility of diagnosing the 6 to 10 percent of children who will be at risk for future psychological problems. Sensitive detection does not occur in the typical surrogate care setting. Professionally trained staff in the public school setting would be able to detect these children and early diagnosis, by age 4 or 5, could prevent the later development of serious problems for many U.S. youngsters.

11 FEDERAL PROGRAMS THAT SERVE CHILDREN AND FAMILIES

Marian Wright Edelman

A nation that continues year after year to spend more money on military defense than on programs of social uplift is approaching spiritual death.

Martin Luther King, Jr.
April 14, 1967

The problem in defense is how far you can go without destroying from within what you are trying to defend from without.

Dwight David Eisenhower
January 19, 1953

In 1983 there were 13.3 million poor children in the United States; 8.5 million of them were white (see Figure 11–1). Since 1979 3.3 million children have fallen into poverty—an increase of 33 percent. A U.S. child has a 1 in 4 chance of being on welfare at some point in his or her lifetime. More than half of all welfare families are white; their average benefit is $3.67 a person a day—53 percent of the poverty level.

Over 12 million children are growing up in female-headed households. Of these 7.2 million are white; their poverty rate is 47 percent. Of the 4.6 million who are black, their poverty rate is 69 percent.

Poverty is the greatest child killer in the affluent United States in the 1980s. More U.S. children die each year from poverty than from traffic fatalities and suicide combined. Twice more children die from

This chapter was adapted from testimony before the Committee on the Budget, U.S. House of Representatives, March 11, 1985.

Figure 11-1. Newly Poor Children in the United States, 1979-83.

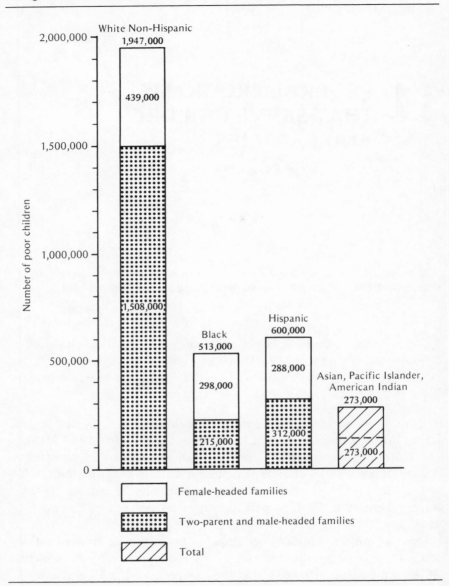

Source: U.S. Department of Commerce, Bureau of the Census, *Current Population Reports*, Series P-60, No. 145, "Money Income and Poverty Status of Families and Persons in the United States: 1983 and preceding volumes. (Advance Data from the March 1984 Current Population Survey)" (Washington, D.C., August 1984), tables 15 and 17.
Calculations by the Children's Defense Fund.

poverty than from cancer and heart disease combined. The Maine child death study estimates 10,000 excess child deaths per year in the United States from poverty-related causes, which exceeds the number of child deaths from cancers and heart diseases combined (Bureau of Health 1983).

Yet for the fifth consecutive year, in the face of the highest child poverty rate in eighteen years, Ronald Reagan has targeted poor children and families again for billions in new budget cuts. Under the fiscal year 1986 Reagan budget, children will lose $5.2 billion. By 1990 children will lose $37.6 billion in federal support. This is beyond the $10 billion a year in cuts already made in survival programs for children and families since 1980.

At the same time, the Reagan budget proposes a $32 billion increase in defense spending in fiscal year 1986 over last year. This is in addition to $178.3 billion in defense increases since 1980. By fiscal year 1990, if the president's defense proposals are carried out, the military budget will increase by another $344.2 billion or 239 percent to make U.S. children more "secure" from external enemies.

CHILDREN NEED DEFENSE FROM
THE ENEMIES WITHIN TOO

U.S. children need defense against the domestic enemy of poverty. Over a five-year period, more U.S. children die from poverty than the total number of U.S. battle deaths in the Vietnam War. Yet national leaders dream about a multibillion dollar Star Wars system to make our defenses impenetrable against enemy missiles. A smaller achievable war could be waged against child poverty—a war that saves and enhances rather than takes and threatens human life. Every poor U.S. child could be lifted out of poverty in 1986 for less than half of the proposed defense spending increase for that year alone.

U.S. babies need defense against preventable infant mortality and birth defects. By 1990, 22,000 U.S. babies will die primarily because of low birthweight. We can prevent at least one in eight of these infant deaths and thousands of handicapping conditions simply by providing their mothers with prenatal care. For 7 percent, or twenty-five days, of the 1986 defense budget increase, every poor mother and baby could be provided Medicaid, and thus prenatal care, coverage. Instead, the Reagan budget proposes to cut Medicaid again by

$6 billion over the next three years, eliminate Migrant Health Centers, and cut services under Maternal and Child Health programs. How many four-pound babies will it take to balance the federal budget?

Tens of thousands of U.S. preschool children need defense against preventable disease. Yet while the president plans to build 17,000 new nuclear weapons over this decade at an estimated cost of $71 billion, his budget allows for only a single month's stockpile of vaccination serum. Two million fewer children will be immunized against DPT next year because of Reagan budget requests that ignore the dramatically increased costs of vaccines and the unmet need. Half of all black preschool children are not fully immunized against DPT and polio.

U.S. children need to be protected against increasing child abuse. Every American supports a strong defense and well-defined national security goals, but children have a similar right to security against sexual and other abuse in day care centers and at home. An estimated 1.5 million children were reported abused and neglected in 1983, an increase of 200,000 children over the previous year. Why then is the Reagan administration cutting funding 15 percent for the only program specifically targeted on the prevention and treatment of child abuse, providing no funding for the recently enacted Family Violence Prevention and Services program, and eliminating a new $25 million child care training fund to prevent child abuse in day care centers?

U.S. children need defense against growing homelessness. According to a 1984 Department of Housing and Urban Development (HUD) study, 22 percent of the homeless population in shelters, not including runaway shelters, is made up of children under age 18. It is estimated that over 66,000 children are currently living without adequate permanent shelter. Rather than seeking to provide decent housing and minimal income supports to help families weather unemployment and loss of shelter, the president's budget seeks to emasculate low-income housing programs and to rip another $325 million hole in the tattered survival net of Aid to Families with Dependent Children (AFDC). The budget for AFDC recipients, 66 percent of whom are children, has already been cut $1.7 billion since 1980. Recipients receive an average daily benefit of $3.67.

Further, U.S. youth need defense against dependency and despair. Our adolescents are dropping out of school only to find that there are no jobs for them and beginning families as teenagers only to find they cannot support them. Today there is

One dropout for every five high school graduates;
One youth actively looking for work and unable to find it for every four who have jobs;
One birth to an unmarried teenager for every four births to married 25- to 29-year-olds.

For all its talk about the U.S. family and the ethic of work, the administration's budget proposes to eliminate the Job Corps, cut the Summer Youth program and student loans, and freeze the educational and child care programs essential for youth opportunity and eventual self-sufficiency.

In sum, the Reagan fiscal year 1986 budget turns its back on the needs of children and adolescents and will make their lives harder. It will push millions more children toward the ragged edge of survival or worse and turn children with potential into youth in trouble.

Governmental actions since 1980 have taken their toll on health, nutrition, child care, and educational opportunity of millions of U.S. children. U.S. children today are significantly poorer, more likely to suffer death and sickness, hunger and homelessness, abuse and neglect, and be denied vital educational assistance, training, and child care than just four years ago.

Black children particularly are sliding backward. Compared to five years ago, they are more likely to be born into poverty, to an adolescent or single mother, and to an unemployed parent, to be unemployed themselves as a teenager, and not to go to college after high school graduation. Because black children are more than twice as likely to be poor as white children, they will be disproportionately affected by the president's proposed budget cuts in programs for children and the poor.

In light of the crisis among our young, the president's budget is inhumane and unfair, but it is also short-sighted and costly. It wastes the precious potential of too many of our nation's young, a long-term price that all of us will continue to pay far into the future. It will also mortgage the future of *all* children. Just the military *increase* alone from fiscal year 1980 to fiscal year 1990 will exceed the federal debt now held by the public by several hundred billion dollars. These debts will burden young men and women for decades. Yet the Reagan administration ignores present and future needs and continues to cut federal programs for children in order to apy for the enormous build-up in defense and tax subsidies for the rich.

The Reagan budget proposes nothing to staunch even a little of the mammoth treasury hemorrhage caused by the tax cut of 1981, which helped the rich at the expense of the poor and contributed to the highest deficits in U.S. history. While the president claims to want the poor to work, he has penalized their work with higher taxes and ignored the skyrocketing federal tax burden on the working poor. The amount of federal tax paid by those with incomes below the federal poverty line increased 58 percent from 1980 to 1982 alone.

A working single mother with three children and a below-poverty income of $10,500 paid a higher federal income and social security tax rate (21 percent) on a salary increase in 1984 than the wealthiest taxpayer paid on profits from the sale of stocks and bonds and real estate (20 percent). Indeed, on her $10,500 income, she paid $1,186 in combined federal taxes, more than Boeing, General Electric, Dupont, Texaco, Mobil, and AT&T paid in total federal income taxes in 1983, although these huge corporations earned $13.7 billion in profits.

The president has touted the Grace Commission's recommendations for deficit reduction through social welfare program cuts. He has been silent about the fact that the W. R. Grace Company earned $684 million profits from 1981 to 1983, paid no net federal income taxes, and received $12.5 million from the government in negative income taxes through rebates or sales of "excess" tax benefits. If we just raised the Grace Company tax rate to *zero*, we could pay for 9 million of the free school lunches President Reagan and the Congress cut from children. But the president proposes to cut $630 million more from child nutrition programs in fiscal year 1986. He is not planning to raise The Grace Company's tax rate.

The U.S. Treasury Department estimates that 15 million baseball tickets each year (one-third of the total sold) and half of all hockey tickets are subsidized through corporate tax deductions. The president has not asked the Congress to change this subsidy. Yet the estimated treasury loss, over $80 million, is enough to finance the Juvenile Justice and Delinquency Prevention program the president has asked Congress to abolish.

The deficit crises—but even more important, fairness and justice— dictate action on the revenue side of the budget. How can we as a nation even consider further budget cuts in child nutrition programs when we continue to subsidize the three-martini business lunch? How can we allow a single mother struggling to support her family on poverty level wages pay more taxes than giant, profitable corporations? How can we attempt to deal with dangerous record-breaking deficits and fail to ask the wealthiest in our country to sacrifice even a little? Leadership and courage are required to tackle the tax loopholes and subsidies that cost us billions in lost revenue and respect for our national budget and our federal tax system.

THE CHILDREN'S SURVIVAL BILL

We know that Congress is trying to develop prudent and economically sound steps to deal with the deficit crisis, but so too must proven, cost-effective steps be taken to rescue children from the crisis they face. It is time to invest in our children and youth before they become ill, are left alone, have a baby, or drop out of school.

At the Children's Defense Fund, we have developed an alternative budget approach, a positive agenda for governmental investment for survival and opportunity as well as for budgetary prudence and strength. It is called the Children's Survival Bill, and it is a legislative agenda for children, adolescents, and families for the Ninety-ninth Congress. Overall, it is a deficit reduction package, with budget savings and revenue measures far exceeding its new investments in children. We are most grateful that Representative George Miller has agreed to sponsor this legislation.

The Children's Survival Bill is based on a sound and simple premise: An investment of scarce resources in our nation's children will protect our nation's future. Offered as a model for positive investment in the United States' children of the 1980s, the Children's Survival Bill outlines a range of specific preventive steps to give young people the skills and employment opportunities to enable them to contribute to, rather than depend on, the community.

Instead of cutting or freezing vital programs for children and youth, we ask that Congress consider our proposals to invest additional funds in the following federal programs that have a proven record of success and are cost-effective as well:

Health programs for mothers and children, like Medicaid and the Maternal and Child Health Block Grant. For every $1 invested in comprehensive prenatal care, $2 is saved in reduced hospitalization rates in the first year alone of an infant's life;

Educational programs like Chapter I with a long history of teaching children to read and compute at a cost of approximately $625 per year compared to the more than $3,000 cost of keeping a child back to repeat a grade;

Child Care and Preschool Programs like Title XX and Head Start— a motivating program for young children with a fifteen-year track record of success. For every $1 invested in Head Start, $3 are returned in reduced public expenditures and increased public receipts because Head Start children are less likely to end up pregnant as teens or on welfare and more likely to enter vocational school, college, or the workforce;

Child Nutrition programs like WIC that study after study has found to be a success, with $3 in reduced health care costs for every $1 invested;

Child abuse programs such as the Child Abuse Prevention and Treatment Program and Child Welfare Services that provide hope and a future to shattered children and families.

The Children's Survival Bill also proposes creative and cost-effective new endeavors for children and adolescents similarly based on prevention. A major strategy designed to alleviate child poverty and strengthen families is the prevention of adolescent pregnancy and the building of youth self-sufficiency;

In 1983, 525,000 babies were born to teen mothers, 10,000 to girls age 14 and under. Over 300,000 of the teens who give birth annually have not completed high school. Thirty-six thousand have not completed the eighth grade. Thirty-one percent of all babies born to teens are paid for by Medicaid at an annual cost of $200 million. Sixty percent of all AFDC mothers had their first child as a teenager.

All of us have a stake in the development of children and youth into productive, self-sufficient adults and families. The Children's Survival Bill proposes small but necessary investments in the youth of today who tomorrow must shoulder our national debt, finance our Social Security, and lead us into the twenty-first century. These investments are more than offset by savings brought about by the elimination of the MX missile and of the unfair tax subsidies for the rich.

Some of the following arguments are used to justify the unjust budget priorities of the Reagan administration:

Deficit reduction must be the first priority. Many in the Congress will say this, but they should convince President Reagan, Defense Secretary Casper Weinberger, and the powerful special interest beneficiaries of federal defense and tax largesse to make this *their* priority before sending poor, handicapped, and homeless children again to the frontlines of a deficit reduction war that no one else is fighting. While we are deeply concerned with reducing the deficit and offer specific deficit reduction proposals in the Children's Survival Bill, we believe that in a democratic, affluent society reducing infant death rates and child poverty and suffering takes precedence over reducing the deficit. Indeed, by reducing child poverty, we will be taking steps to curb long-term public costs.

Programs for children and poor families must contribute like all others to reducing the federal deficit. Since 1980 we have cut federal programs for children in order to pay for defense and tax cuts disproportionately targeted to corporations and individual taxpayers who have no minor children or who do not need the tax relief to support their children. And the deficit has grown bigger and bigger. Those who have caused the deficit must cure it. Children and the poor who have been unfairly hurt by disproportionate cuts should be made whole.

A freeze is the fair approach to curbing federal spending and controlling the deficit. President Reagan is not proposing to freeze most children's programs: he is proposing to eliminate or cut them deeply—again. He is not proposing to freeze defense; he is proposing to increase it dramatically. He is not proposing to freeze the tax breaks of rich individuals or corporations. Moreover, to freeze children's programs would be to freeze the injustice, suffering, hunger, homelessness, and abuse that previous budget cuts have caused or exacerbated. And that is not fair.

We cannot afford to increase successful children's programs as outlined in the Children's Survival Bill. Of course we can. If we can afford $3.5 billion for forty-eight new MX missiles, we can afford a new $100 million demonstration program to support more comprehensive school-based health clinics to help keep teens from getting pregnant and dropping out of school. That is less than one MX missile. In fact, the savings gained from cancelling *just one MX missile* could alternatively be used to:

Lift 100,000 children out of poverty;

Pay for the entire child abuse prevention state grant program for the next decade;

Provide complete prenatal care for every woman who will give birth with late or no prenatal care next year (about 200,000 women each year);

Pay for a WIC supplemental nutritional package each month for every low-birth-weight infant born next year (about 250,000 infants each year);

Provide four years of Chapter I compensatory education to each of the 60,000 14- and 15-year-old students who will drop out of school next year.

In fact, we cannot afford *not* to invest adequately in children. To continue to give Head Start to only one-sixth of the eligible children—when we know that every $1 invested in Head Start will net us $7 in the long run and $3 in the short run by reducing special education placements and grade retentions and by freeing the parents of Head Start students to work—is poor deficit reduction policy. Yet 19,000 fewer children will receive Head Start next year or the program's quality will be reduced if Reagan budget requests prevail.

Powerful constituencies lack a stake in children's programs and won't support funding increases. *Every* American has a self-interest in investing in *every* child. The military, the private sector, and government need a strong pool of healthy, trained young people. Children, the middle-aged, and the elderly need each other. Social security and Medicare may lessen my stake in my own children's economic future, but it magnifies my stake in the economic future of all children—those who will be paying taxes to support me in my old age. The intergenerational compact is not merely between us as workers and the older generation as dependents, but between us as future retirees and all children as future workers. To protect ourselves in old age, we will need today's and tomorrow's children to be both productive and compassionate. It can only make sense, then, to rebuild a sense of societal responsibility for the nurturing of children. Those children whose parents cannot support them are just as important to me economically as those whose parents can. And to preserve their economic futures—and thereby to protect mine—I must get the society to invest money now. In the year 2000—only 15 years from now—there will be more elderly people per worker as the country becomes an increasingly aging society. Each worker's productivity and contribution becomes more important to all Americans. Those workers are now our children, one-fifth of whom start their lives in abject poverty.

Nothing works. Millions of elderly citizens and children escaped poverty in the 1960s and 1970s. Black and white high school graduates started to enter college in equal numbers. In the fifteen years before Medicaid began, black infant mortality dropped 10 percent. In the decade following Medicaid, it dropped 50 percent. Although we gave compensatory education to fewer than half of those who needed it, in the 1970s we eliminated 40 percent of the gap in reading achievement between black and white elementary school children. A million handicapped children are no longer excluded from school thanks to the Education for All Handicapped Children's Act. And millions of children escaped days of hunger because school lunches and breakfasts and food stamps were provided. These were intrinsically worthwhile investments even if they did not eliminate poverty.

Carefully targeted investment in social welfare programs for children creates long-term savings that more than offset short-term costs. Family planning services, genetic screening at birth with followup treatment for common problems, preventive care, and vaccinations for children—each of these saves many times its cost.

We do not believe that the U.S. public will indefinitely tolerate unnecessary waste. We are wasting lives and money and potential, however, when five-sixths of the children needing Head Start do not get it or when hundreds of thousands of pregnant women receive late or no prenatal care.

Growth is the answer to poverty. Economic growth is critically important to the alleviation of poverty. But economic growth alone is not enough to lift 13.3 million children from poverty. The Reagan economic recovery has been accompanied by increases rather than decreases in the ranks of the poor and unemployed. Just as liberals must pay more attention to growth and productivity issues, conservatives must pay more attention to the need for federal investment in targeted jobs and training policies for unemployed youth and adults; for child care and other support services to enable mothers to work;

and for income supports for those for whom work is not available. And we must ensure that barriers of race, sex, and handicap are removed for all those who need work.

The budget process drives the nation's priorities at home and abroad. It is our national Rorschach test. How well hungry children in Mississippi and Ethiopia will be fed, whether we will finance just or repressive regimes in Latin America, whether our nuclear arsenal will continue to grow or shrink, are affected significantly by the budget decisions made by Congress.

President Reagan wants to invest over $3.2 trillion dollars over this decade in the military and in new eapons of death of no use to the hungry children of this world. We want to invest in new weapons of life: education, health care, family support, jobs, and food. President Reagan wants to protect big corporations from federal taxes; we want to protect poor working mothers and fathers. President Reagan is trying to take away school lunches, immunizations, and health care from poor children; we are campaigning for a right to prenatal care so that every baby can have a healthy beginning. We believe ours is a just and sound budget approach.

Children and adolescents don't vote or lobby or make campaign contributions. They do not come to Washington to demonstrate or visit offices or even write letters about the budget. But children and youth are the nation's real national security. They are also the most cost-effective investment a nation can make toward assuring its future and strong democratic leadership for the rest of the world.

REFERENCE

Bureau of Health, Maine Department of Human Services, Childhood Death and Poverty. 1983. *A Study of All Childhood Deaths in Maine, 1976-80*. Augusta, Maine: Bureau of Health, Maine Department of Human Services, Childhood Death and Poverty. April.

12 PROGRESS, SO VERY SLOW

Eli Ginzberg

Both governmental and private sectors have been very slow in creating family policy that facilitates the special needs of children and parents. Almost a decade and a half ago President Nixon vetoed the comprehensive legislation that Congress passed to strengthen child care programs. The grounds that Nixon gave for vetoing the bill provided a prelude of things to come. He pointed out that the legislation favored the intrusion of government into an area that had long been the preserve of parents—a move that he considered undesirable and unwise. He also noted that if the bill became law it would lead to a "new army of bureaucrats"—a trend that he felt would not be beneficial. Moreover, the president emphasized that the eventual costs of the new services covered in the legislation would soon be many times greater than the initial authorization. Finally, he believed that existing government programs should provide new and improved social services for children.

One way to explain why the vetoed bill was not reintroduced and passed under a later president, particularly under the Democratic president Jimmy Carter, is that the Mondale-sponsored bill of 1971 was a "fluke": It passed through the House and the Senate without a broad national consensus, and Nixon's veto provided the time and impetus for opponents to mobilize themselves to assure that if reintroduced it would fail. A related explanation is that the 1971 passage was the final piece of the Great Society legislation that passed

117

through the Congress and that once vetoed, the momentum for wide-ranging social reform was spent.

Finally, the deterioration in federal finances with the unbroken string of deficits must be taken into account. Nixon was doubtless correct when he emphasized that if the child care bill became law the long-term costs would mount rapidly. The adverse turn in the nation's economy and in the complexities facing the federal government with inflation, the end of dollar conversion, and price and wage controls could also be seen as new and unscalable barriers.

The Nixon veto did not result in total nonparticipation of the federal government in expanded funding for child care. Congress became increasingly interested in facilitating the employment of female heads of households on Aid to Families with Dependent Children (AFDC) and to that end made considerable funds available for child care under Title XX of the Social Security Act, a considerable part of which was used by the states to support child care centers. In 1981, as part of the Reagan tax reform package, child care costs up to $4,860 per year became eligible for a tax credit of up to $1,400 for two or more children, depending on family adjusted gross income.

The states and the localities depended on federal dollars for social interventions in the 1960s and looked to Washington to take the lead in any significant new funding for child care services. When the lead was not forthcoming, they remained largely passive. In a small number of states, and in a few localities, nonfederal tax revenues were appropriated in small amounts to encourage the establishment and expansion of child care facilities, primarily to assist women on welfare or in lower income brackets in maintaining employment.

But state and local governments hesitated to become heavily involved in providing their own dollars for more child care services because of resistance from taxpayers and because of annual per-child costs of around $3,500 to $4,500 for quality care—more than double the cost that many parents paid for informal neighborhood day care. Costs and prices are much higher for professionally sponsored and approved centers that require good physical facilities, high personnel ratios, and good nutritional and health care services than they are for informal arrangements under which a neighbor accepts responsibility for caring and feeding of one or more youngsters while their mothers are at work. Many mothers feel that a neighbor will provide more reliable care than a larger, more impersonal center. The proximity of the neighbor's home is an important additional benefit in terms of drop-off and collection.

The original concern of government centered on the provision of child care for low-income and welfare families, particularly those with a female head of household. Aside from the state and federal interest in reducing the welfare rolls and reducing the burdens on taxpayers, this early focus was reinforced by the fact that relatively few middle-class women with children under age 3 were in the labor market. In 1975, the earliest year for which data are available, one-third of women with children under age 3 were in the labor force; today almost half of such mothers are in the labor force. This substantial and rapid shift in the proportion of working mothers with very young children goes far to explain why Congress adopted a liberal child care expenditures provision in its tax revisions of 1981. Many observers of funding policy note that what was once an issue limited to the poor or the single mother has been transformed into a middle-class issue. Half of all married women with children under age 6 are in the labor market.

It is reasonable to hypothesize that if the conditions of the mid-1960s prevailed today—with broad public support for social programming and a favorable federal budgetary outlook—Congress would be likely to increase its appropriations for child care services. But an electorate skeptical about governmental programs and a federal deficit that threatens to worsen rather than to improve are not likely to convince Congress to assist families in obtaining more and better child care services. If anything, the large numbers of parents who would avail themselves of such services if they were provided is a deterrent to congressional action in the present circumstances. Although the budgetary position of most states is superior to that of the federal government, most states would find the raising of substantial additional revenue difficult—and that is what they would have to do if they responded broadly to the child care issue. Progress in child care has been slow for more than economic reasons, but the money issue goes far to explain why all levels of government have resisted becoming more heavily involved in child care.

The nongovernmental sector, particularly business, trade unions, and religious and eleemosynary organizations, have to some extent responded to the needs of a rapidly changing society with altered patterns of employment and child care and family services. Compared to the advanced nations in Western Europe, the United States has moved only a short distance to provide maternity leaves, with and without pay, for working women and has for the most part ignored fathers. Although many employers make informal arrangements with selected women employees that may cover leaves for as long as a year and on occasion even longer, most contractual arrangements are usually for no more than a few months and frequently without pay.

Until recently, most U.S. women workers who were about to have a child withdrew from the labor force either permanently or for a period of years—so that it was impractical for an employer to keep a job open or to assure the returnee an alternative position. The absence of monetary benefits connected with childbirth in the United States reflects a program of health care coverage that is less comprehensive than that of the countries of Western Europe, less interest in pronatal policies, and a different set of priorities among trade union members and leaders. These deficiencies lead to the absence in the United States of any strong advocacy for child care allowances programs that have had much support in European countries, particularly in France, the United Kingdom, the Netherlands, and Sweden.

Two observations suggest themselves. A child allowance program that makes a significant transfer of resources to families with children on an entitlement basis places unacceptable burdens on taxpayers so that such programs seldom make a significant difference in the resources available to families with children. The alternative approach gears child allowances to income needs, which makes such a program differ only slightly from the current practice of adjusting welfare and public assistance programs to the numbers of children that the needy household must support.

There is no question that the United States lags considerably behind most of the other OECD countries with respect to maternity leaves, maternity payments, and child care allowances and related benefits. There has been relatively little employee pressure in the United States for such benefits via the private arena, but the European child allowance schemes have had in most countries only a marginal effect on easing the financial predicament of families with children.

The availability and financing of child care facilities—defined as opportunities for working women (and a few working men) to leave their preschool children in a supervised environment—have increased.

Recent decades have witnessed a growth in most urban areas of government-sponsored and privately sponsored child care facilities, mostly for children between ages 3 to 5, and some communities use a sliding scale of fees depending on parental income and parental service contribution. By and large, employers have been slow to establish and operate child care facilities with the exception of a few special institutions such as hospitals, and trade unions have been equally slow—for reasons of cost, complexity, and uncertain demand for the service (if mothers are disinclined to have their young children travel to and from a center that is far from their homes).

Employers have not wanted to include child care as an employee benefit because of its high cost and the relatively small numbers of employees who need and want it, although a few large corporations have moved to cafeteria benefits that include child care as an option. IBM provides informational services for employees to help them find alternative sources of organized child care in their communities. Despite the rapid growth of employment among women with preschool children, however, the business community, including the most profitable corporations, has been very slow to move into the child care arena. The trade union movement expresses support for more and better employer-financed child care services but has not been willing to expend its limited chips on turning words into actions.

We find therefore a low level of organized response by the powerful private sector parties—business and labor—to speed the growth of child care facilities. This fact, added to the economic barriers to expanded government financing, suggests that the United States will rely on ad hoc approaches to narrow the gap between new employment lifestyles and institutional supports. The bulk of child care probably will continue for many years to be provided by private arrangements between parents and relatives and neighbors.

The complexity of the problem and the slowness of progress to date can be better appreciated by noting some additional facts. The most difficult is that with half of all mothers of children under age 3 in the labor force, there is a growing need for care of infants and toddlers. It is generally acknowledged that institutional care for infants is among the most difficult and costly of all child care arrangements, yet the demand for infant care is rising.

Another difficulty is the problem of "latch-key" children. These are school-age youngsters from ages 5 to 12 who are unsupervised from 2:30 or 3 P.M. when school lets out until a parent arrives home, which is frequently not before 6 P.M. These youngsters often remain unsupervised on days when school is not in session and their parents are working, particularly during the long summer vacation.

The French have used the *école maternelle* to provide a combination of early childhood education with child care supervision for a large proportion of their entire child population, starting at around 2, and coverage tends to coincide with the parents' workday. Support is growing for the adaptation of the French system to the United States, intensified by an increasing concern to improve the educability of all our youth, but progress along this route is certain to be slow. It depends on state leadership, on local school board support on taxpayer approval, and on a reassessment of the public school system so that urban schools would not be patronized exclusively by the children of low-income families.

The most probable next step toward this goal is to expand kindergarten in public schools so that all children have the opportunity to start at age 4. Today only half of all eligible children in communities attend kindergarten. But a 4-year-old cannot remain in kindergarten all day unless the program has been expanded to include feeding, rest, playtime, and much more. The cost of such a broadened program comes high.

It is not difficult to understand why progress has been slow in making suitable child care services available to all families. The federal, state, and local governments and business have been unable or unwilling to assume on behalf of the taxpayer or the stockholder the substantial costs of expanding these services to a level that would meet the latent demand and provide services of acceptable quality.

Their fiscal resistance has been strengthened by the perception that, despite strong advocacy on the part of some groups, the public at large does not feel that it has a major stake in the broadening of child care services. Most voters and most taxpayers do not face the problem of caring for young children. Further, the nation's politicians and businesspeople recognize that current institutional and individual arrangements meet the most pressing needs of parents. Large numbers of individual children are not receiving the quality of services that could make an optimal contribution to their development, and some are being abused. The extant system, however, appears to be performing no worse, if no better, than most societal arrangements.

Advocates for change make an important point. The family as we have known it—with a working father and a mother at home with primary responsibility for overseeing the rearing of the children—is no longer prototypical. In fact, it is the exception. It will not be long before the majority of mothers even of very young children—those under age 3—will be in the labor force. The development of children has been a shared responsibility between family and society for centuries, ever since publicly financed education was first established. As work and lifestyles shift, the nature of this societal responsibility must also shift. The proper care for and the development of children remains a primary responsibility of parents—but not of parents alone. Only a society that has lost its bearings would risk neglecting to contribute—and liberally—to ensuring that the oncoming generation has the benefit of a good start in life.

13 EMPLOYEE BENEFITS AND ASSISTANCE TO WORKING PARENTS

Dallas L. Salisbury
Hazel A. Witte

Workers in the United States are accustomed to receiving employee benefits as an indirect means of providing for their economic well-being, health, and safety; benefits have been a part of employment packages for the last fifty years. Employers have come to view such benefits as enhancing worker productivity and satisfaction. Both management and labor, under various regulatory schemes of the federal and state governments, have accepted the central role played by employee benefits in maintaining the postindustrial U.S. economy. According to Patrick J. Scollard, executive vice president, Chemical Bank,

> The dramatic change in the work force as well as the family structure means that our nation and the private sector must place a high priority in understanding the problems faced by workers, in order to create family-oriented benefits for an increasingly diverse work force in the United States. Allowing much greater choices for individuals with different needs will undoubtedly be a key to many of the solutions in the years ahead (Scollard 1986).

The U.S. employee benefit pattern has evolved to include health coverage, retirement income plans, job-related disability programs, and employer-subsidized life insurance. These features are the core

The views expressed in this paper are those of the authors and should not be attributed to the Employee Benefit Research Institute, its officers, trustees, sponsors, or other staff.

of indirect employment compensation for individuals, and they ultimately filter down to benefit the families of workers.

Many employee benefits are mandated by law, such as employer
contributions to social security, Medicare, unemployment insurance,
and workers' compensation insurance. Recent legislation requires
employers with group health coverage to provide terminated employees, spouses, and certain family members the chance to continue
health care coverage at 102 percent of group rates.[1] These programs
have been established to protect the working, nonworking, and
retired against financial disaster. Social security and Medicare benefit
provisions for spouses also affect family financial obligations and
security, including those of eligible divorced spouses.

Other employee benefits are discretionary and serve different goals
and receive different tax treatment. Benefits that help employees to
meet special needs or insure against financial risks are most often
tax exempt. Tax-exempt employee benefits include employer contributions to health insurance, child care, and employer cost for the
first $50,000 of group life health insurance. These benefits often per-
mit families to take advantage of the lower rates and broader policies
of group coverage that for single purchasers either cost more or are
unavailable. The scale of family involvement is especially apparent
in health insurance coverage. More than 60 percent of the civilian
U.S. population was covered by an employer group health insurance
plan at some time during 1977 (Chollet 1984: 7). More than half
of all persons with employer group coverage are insured as dependents of covered workers.

Retirement income employee benefit programs help protect employees against income loss at retirement and encourage retirement
planning during the employee's worklife. In May 1983 pension coverage rates for employer-sponsored plans was 52 percent (Andrews
1985).

The 1984 Retirement Equity Act permits broader spousal access
to pension funds. Ex-spouses may also have a claim to pension and
survivor benefits if the court awards that right. The Retirement
Equity Act also reduces participation age and vesting requirements,
which particularly affect women workers.

Direct family supportive benefits, such as on-site child care, have
a long, erratic history dating from the Civil War and the influx of
female workers in the textile and clothing factories. Recent governmental inducements in favor of family-oriented benefits have resulted

in tax advantages for employers who provide specialized benefit packages. Such tax advantages are creating an uneven, still-developing configuration of child care, maternity and paternity leave, employee assistance plans, flexible benefit plans, and other benefit package combinations.

Governmental programs are directed at families whose occupational and employment circumstances render them more marginal to the private sector workforce. For the 6 million workers employed directly by government, employee benefits have begun to resemble packages offered by private employers.

For the past twenty years employers have viewed family benefits as a recruitment tool and have developed benefit programs to give concrete expression to their social responsibility commitments. Some observers point out that new workforce realities—such as large numbers of women in the workforce and the trend toward dual-earner families—have made family benefits the essential new element of twenty-first-century employment.

FAMILY BENEFITS AND THE "NEW" U.S. WORKFORCE

The massive shift of U.S. women from the home into the labor force has brought their needs and problems into the employment limelight. This is especially true of so-called pink-collar workers (female lower-level office workers moving from homemaking careers to regular, salaried employment).

By 1990 10.4 million U.S. children under age 6 will have working mothers ("Child Care Programs" 1985: 1). This is double the number of preschool children whose mothers worked in 1970 and is the result of economic imperatives and the post-World War II jump in population. Sixty percent of married mothers with children age 5 and younger are presently in the workforce, up from 37 percent in 1970 ("Child Care Programs" 1985: 1). In addition, more than a quarter of all families with children have only one parent present. It is clear that family obligations significantly affect the workforce.

Working parents are expected to comprise more than 66 percent of the U.S. workforce in 1990 (Child Care Systems, Inc. 1985: 1) and family care and child care problems increasingly condition the workplace. Child care is a common concern for most employers. One experience typically shared by employers is the heavy toll taken on paid-time benefits by family responsibilities. It is not unusual for parents, especially working mothers and single parents, to use vacation time, sick leave, and personal days to cope with child care problems. The need for child care prompts thousands of workers annually to move from full-time to part-time employment, partly due to the expense or unreliability of child care arrangements. Costs of child care can devour half a parent's take-home pay. Dependable, well-trained child care services are in short supply: It is estimated that the 1985 national demand for full-time preschool and after-school child care exceeded by 5 million children the available places for them in child-serving agencies.

In a 1984 study by Child Care Systems, Inc., 51 percent of working parents made new child care arrangements one or more times during a twelve-month period, spending an average of 9.8 hours on each change. Of the 1,888 parents surveyed in CCS, Inc.'s national study of child care arrangements, 28 percent said they are late to work or leave work early twice a month or more because of child care problems (Child Care Systems, Inc. 1985: 4–5).

THE UPWARDLY MOBILE, BABY-BOOM FAMILY

Workers between ages 25 and 40 are now involved in the workforce as dual-earning parents at levels unprecedented since World War II. In addition, substantial numbers of women in their late 20s and 30s are just beginning their families. Both employers and the workers of this age group are heavily invested in educational preparation and advanced on-the-job technical training. And this workforce segment is expected to cope effectively with child care and other family problems.

Experience and studies disclose that these parents have new preferences for the structure of employee benefit policies. In order to combine work and family into a minimally harmonious existence, this particular age group is seeking flexible work hours, cafeteria-style benefits, parental leaves, employer-provided child care help, and less rigid relocation policies (*Wall Street Journal* 1985: 1). Federal initiatives have provided incentives for including family-oriented benefits within the scope of employee benefits, but they have largely run their course, in part due to budget deficit problems.

FEDERAL POLICY AND PRIVATE INITIATIVE

Some national policies, of course, continue to spur private sector experimentation with family-oriented employee benefits. One important example is the Pregnancy Discimination Act of 1978. While it mandated no particular benefits, the act prohibited discrimination against pregnant workers. The scheme of the act is simple: It designated such discrimination illegal and added a new category to the civil rights guaranteed under statute by the Constitution. Employers began crafting human resource policies to avoid sex discrimination suits and began considering a host of family-oriented benefits policies such as paternity leave, flextime, part-time employment, job sharing arrangements, as well as traditional child care services.

Some of these policies may be merely temporary solutions. Each has unique advantages and disadvantages, the testing of which discloses differing employer evaluations across the United States. Job sharing arrangements, for example, can create labor relations problems for employers and may be in vogue with employees one year but in disfavor the next. However, the search for employer assistance benefiting both the family and the workforce appears to be a permanent characteristic of employer and trade union decisionmaking.

MATERNITY LEAVE AND BENEFITS

The Pregnancy Discrimination Act of 1978, which amended Title VII of the Civil Rights Act of 1964, mandates employers with short-term disability plans to treat disability due to pregnancy and childbirth in the same manner as other disabilities. Employers who do not offer short-term disability plans are not required to offer maternity disability. California, Hawaii, New Jersey, New York, and Rhode Island have laws requiring employers to provide short-term disability benefits, which include benefits for pregnancy-related disabilities.

A few states require employers to grant special disability leave for pregnancy-related conditions, even if the same leave is not given to other temporarily disabled employees. A recent case now under consideration in the Supreme Court upheld state law providing special disability leave for pregnancy, finding that equality under the Pregnancy Discrimination Act must be measured in terms of employment opportunity, not necessarily in amounts of money expended or in the number of days of disability leave expended.[2]

Increasingly, companies are examining their maternity policies for reasons other than compliance with state and national disability initiatives. Ninety percent of working women are of childbearing age, and 80 percent are expected to become pregnant during their working lives; by 1990 women will equal 50 percent of the workforce. Worklife expectancies for women have increased significantly, while men's worklife expectancies have dropped (Silverman 1985: 15). It is imperative for effective management to plan workforce utilization and benefit assistance for intermittent breaks in service due to pregnancy.

If offered, the types of maternity leave commonly fall into three basic categories: disability, paid leave beyond disability, and unpaid leave. Disability leave includes some salary replacement as well as certification of disability by a physician. The average length of disability leave for pregnancy is six to eight weeks. Most often the percentage of salary paid is based on length of service rather than on the job rank or position.

Some employers do offer maternity leave at full salary. Of the large companies that offer full salary, one in four do so for sixteen weeks or less,[3] with financial companies having the highest proportion of companies paying full salary. Many employers offer a combination of full and partial paid leaves, usually up to four months.

Unpaid leave is the most common type of maternity policy, with a variety of time limitations for return to work. Under all three types of leave, it is implicitly recognized that vacation and accrued sick leave and personnel leave may be applied, though use of these benefits can be limited by explicitly stated personnel policies or labor contracts.

Another facet of maternity leave is the retention of benefits during the leave. The most desirable situation for both employers and employee is to continue benefits during leave time. However, some company policies provide partial benefits or continue benefits with additional cost to the employee.

Another approach to maternity leave is to allow workers to return to work part-time during a short period after the leave. A gradual return to the job may be more valuable than a lengthy leave and, in combination with continuing benefits, may be the most desirable leave policy. The gradual return may be especially important to the adjustment period of the employee and family both in terms of health and child care arrangements.

Job guarantees are also crucial to implementing maternity leave policies. A California state law that requires employers to offer a woman returning from maternity leave the same or similar job, though men on disability leave received no similar guarantee, was recently upheld by the U.S. Court of Appeals, Ninth Circuit.[4] The majority of companies offering job guarantees usually do so for not more than four months.

PATERNITY LEAVE

Child care has become an important concern for men as well as for women. Fewer firms offer leave that is specifically paternity leave, though the number is growing and has been an issue in some recent bargaining contracts. Most paternity leaves are unpaid, though the use of vacation time and accrued sick leave and personal leave is available within the confines of personnel policies and labor contracts. A recent consent decree of the U.S. Equal Employment Opportunity Commission, provided a leave provision in a collective bargaining contract that allowed nondisabled women to take leave following birth could not be denied to a male employee who wanted paternity leave.

Companies that explicitly offer paternity leave may implicitly discourage its use through internal pressures and expectations. The company or occupational culture may affect actual usage of paternity leave more than mere availability of the leave.

ADOPTION LEAVE

The number of employers that offer adoption leave and benefits is growing, and the impetus for developing such leave policies seems to come from the companies themselves. It is a low-cost benefit that generates a substantial amount of goodwill. The existence of adoption leave and benefits also promotes a parity between natural and adoptive parents as to the cost of adding to a family and the amount of time for adjustment.

Adoption benefits range from $150 to $2,500 for covered expenses, such as agency placement fees, legal, and court fees. Cash benefits for adoption are considered part of the employee's income, which reduces by up to 25 percent the net amount that parents receive, unless companies choose to accept the income tax burden. The Economic Recovery Tax Act of 1981 did provide a deduction of up to $1,500 for the adoption of a "special needs" child (one who is age 5 or older, handicapped, or a sibling set).[5]

In addition, approximately 100 firms allow employees to use accrued leave time and sometimes sick leave for adoption purposes. Such leave can be crucial for the many cases in which adoption agencies stipulate that parents arrange to take a specified amount of leave from their jobs to care for the adopted child.

CHILD CARE BENEFITS

In order to study how child care is shaped by employee benefits programs, it is necessary to separate parental from employer preferences for child care and family tax benefits. The overwhelming parental preference for young children is for in-home child care. According to a 1982 Census Bureau study, 80 percent of employed mothers surveyed used in-home child care or family care for their youngest child under age 5 (U.S. Department of Commerce 1983: 5). The underground economy that exists for child care cannot be underestimated. Caretakers in private homes are often unlicensed and frequently prefer cash payments. Such cash arrangements are acceptable to parents who feel that they are receiving good and/or affordable child care and are willing to sacrifice the tax credit available to them for child care expenses. Families who use unlicensed child care also may be precluded from using employer child care benefits, which commonly will pay only for licensed care (EBRI 1985).

By far the most important child care funding is the federal tax credit allowed for dependent care under the Internal Revenue Code, section 21(a). Parents may claim the credit for care of children under age 15 when both spouses work full-time or when one spouse works part-time or is a student. The qualified expenses are limited to $2,400 for one child and $4,800 for two or more children but cannot exceed the earned income of the individual, if single, or the earned income of the spouse with the lower earnings for married couples.

A credit equal to 30 percent of eligible expenses is available to individuals with adjusted gross incomes of $10,000 or less, with the credit reduced by one percentage point for each $2,000 of income between $10,000 and $28,000. For individuals with adjusted gross incomes above $28,000, the credit is limited to 20 percent of qualified expenses.

If the employer decides to offer child care benefits, it may offer a variety of approaches, including on-site or near-site care, family day care support, after-school day care support, information and referral, financial assistance in the form of vouchers or discounts, and flexible spending accounts. Although few employers have embraced child care programs as an employee benefit, interest is growing. The development of on-site or near-site programs have an uneven history, with present utilization rates ranging from 4 to 10 percent of employees at a given time. The cost and potential liabilities with on-site day care are a concern experienced by all day care centers, but successful on-site centers are valuable to the employer because they decrease the rate of employee turnover and absenteeism, heighten morale and motivation, and increase the ability to attract employees. On-site centers are especially valuable in settings such as hospitals, where the work hours are irregular and there is an incentive to keep skilled personnel.

Family day care, which is preferred by parents of small children, is difficult for employers to support. Flexible spending accounts or employer-sponsored information and referral, perhaps in tandem with state and local agencies, may provide some support for family day care. But even simple referrals may open the employer to liability problems. Some employers have recognized the shortage of licensed available child care workers, and consortiums, notably in the San Francisco area, provide financial support for training licensed child care workers.

The voucher and discount system can apply to both family day care support and group care, such as nursery schools and after school programs. Under this system, the employer gives workers a day care allowance that permits them to chose the arrangements. This type of system is well suited to areas with established quality day care and referral networks.

After-school child care assistance, other than the voucher and discount system, has not stimulated employer interest. Some view it as a state and municipal responsibility, since many after-school programs are school-based. Nevertheless, it is an area of rapidly changing funding, where there is room for future cooperative activity among all levels of government and the private sector ("Child Care Programs" 1985: 6).

Child care benefits from the employer must be offered as a qualified dependent care assistance program under section 129 of the Internal Revenue Code. Such programs are subject to the nondiscrimination and eligibility rules of the overall benefit plan. The value of the benefits may be excluded from the employee's taxable income and therefore is not eligible for the individual income tax credit for child care. Deductible amounts, if paid by the employee, are eligible for the federal tax credit.

Flexible spending accounts are reimbursement accounts often used to fund benefits in a cafeteria-style plan (Internal Revenue Code Section 125). The plan may be funded through salary reduction, employer contributions, or both. Employees were once able to take claims for reimbursement of expenses from one unallocated credit pool, and at year's end take the unused credits in cash, roll them into the next year's credit pool, or place in a qualified deferred compensation plan. Due to Internal Revenue Service restrictions to "use or lose" the funds within the year, the popularity of this type of plan has diminished.

FLEXIBLE BENEFITS

Flexible benefit plans allow employees to choose among a variety of benefit options paid for by employer contributions or salary reduction. Most often the employer provides a minimum level of certain basic benefits, such as medical, life insurance, disability, pensions, and vacation, and a second level of coverage in the form of benefit credits. Employees use the credits to purchase additional basic benefit coverage or benefits in other areas. Other plans may permit the employee to chose among several levels of core benefits or among several predetermined benefit packages ("Introducing Flexible Benefits" 1985: 25).

Flexible benefit plans allow the employee to tailor a benefit package that at least partially accommodates individual preferences. Flexible benefits have long been considered helpful by a substantial number of employees and by employers who offer such plans in order to better manage benefit cost, meet employee needs, or redesign programs. Such plans can offer options that are important to employees and their families at particular times in their lives, such as child care, hearing and eye care, dental care, and legal services. It also helps families avoid duplicating benefit coverage between wage earners.

The appeal of flexible benefits for employers is cost control and for employees it is the ability to tailor benefits to meet needs. This type of control may be particularly suited to professionals and managers who want more control and options for fiscal matters and tax planning. Hourly and clerical employees may be more cautious about benefit flexibility and may choose to retain comprehensive company-sponsored benefits. By allowing payment options for chosen benefits, however, this type of plan may offer these employees more control of out-of-pocket expenditures (Goldfarb 1986: 98).

FLEXIBLE WORK POLICIES

Flexible human resource policies, such as flextime, part-time work, job sharing, and flexible leave policies, may reduce the need for extensive child care. Such policies are also a method for meeting temporary needs, such as maternity leave or sick child leave, yet allow continued use of a valuable employee.

Part-time employment can be a benefit problem for employers. Legally required employer payments of benefits are almost 30 percent of employee benefits, which means that every employee is automatically more costly thant he wage he or she takes home. Nearly two-thirds of voluntary benefits take the form of paid vacation and sick leave.

Prorating benefits is typically offered as a solution to the problem of paying for expensive benefits such as health and pension. But administrative tasks for keeping track of vested workers is burdensome for defined benefit plans and health insurers prefer employers with a broad risk pool. Employees who have prorated benefits and pay a large amount to continue themselves and dependents under a plan may be viewed as an adverse selection problem, whereby riskier employees are most likely to choose expensive health items.

Adverse selection is not an overriding concern for flexible benefit plans, since adverse selection is expected, and prorating benefit dollars for part-time workers may be less of a problem. In addition, defined contribution plans or 401k (qualified cash or deferred arrangement under section 401k of the Internal Revenue Code) may be made available to part-time employees without the administrative problems of defined benefit plans.

CONCLUSION

Employee benefit plans that offer health, life, and disability insurance as well as vacation leave developed out of public and private concerns for the welfare of the worker, and by addressing some of the needs of the worker's family they eventually became a component of labor and management activity. Changes in the composite of the workforce as well as in the family structure itself stimulated additional activity in the area of family-oriented benefits, such as flexible benefit programs, alternative work schedules, additional dental and vision provisions to health insurance, and child care. Employers who offer benefits that affect families must accurately assess employee needs in order to identify the services that can best serve the plan population.

The workforce is in constant change, and so benefit plans will change as well. Today a variety of benefit strategies are available to meet the needs of working families. The choice for both employer and employee strategies depends on their creating possible solutions to problems and anticipating the consequences of these solutions.

NOTES

1. Title X, Consolidated Omnibus Budget Reconciliation Act, P.L. 99-272.
2. *California Federal Savings & Loan Association v. Guerra*, 84-S843 and 84-S844 (U.S. Sup. Ct. April 15, 1985) (rev. granted).

3. Survey of 153 human resource professionals by *Personnel Administration* magazine (June 1985).
4. *EEOC v. Commonwealth Edison Co.*, USDC NI 11, No. 85, G–S637 (June 28, 1985).
5. Section 222 of the Internal Revenue Code with reference to "special needs child" as defined in section 473 (c) of the Social Security Act.

REFERENCES

Andrews, Emily S. 1985. *The Changing Profiles of Pensions in America.* Washington, D.C.: Employee Benefit Research Institute.

"Child Care Programs and Developments." 1985. *Issue Brief 42.* Washington, D.C.: Employee Benefit Research Institute, May.

Child Care Systems, Inc. 1985. *Preliminary Report on the Workplace Impact of Working Parents.* Lansdale, Penn.: Child Care Systems, Inc.

Chollet, Deborah. 1984. *Employer Provided Health Benefits.* Washington, D.C.: Employee Benefit Research Institute.

"Finances Are Key to After-School Child Care." 1985. *New York Times* (September 16): A1.

Fundamentals of Employee Benefits, 2 ed. 1985. Washington, D.C.: Employee Benefit Research Institute.

Goldfarb, Steve. 1986. "Benefits of the Future from the Perspective of Employees." *Compensation and Benefits Management* 2 (2) (Winter): 97–100.

"Introducing Flexible Benefits: Three Cases." *Benefit News Analysis* 7 (4) (April): 22–25.

The Pregnancy Discrimination Act of 1978. 1978. Amended section VII of the Civil Rights Act of 1964.

Scollard, Patrick J. 1986. Letter to the Economic Policy Council of the United Nations Association of the United States of America, Washington, D.C. February 12.

Silverman, Phyllis. 1985. "Re-examining Maternity Leave." *National Underwriter* (April 13): 15.

U.S. Department of Commerce, Bureau of the Census. 1983. "Child Care Arrangements of Working Mothers." *Current Population Reports*, ser. P–23 (June).

14 THE MALE/FEMALE EARNINGS DIFFERENTIAL IN BRITAIN AND EUROPE
Are There Lessons for the United States?

Peter J. Sloane

In the United Kingdom there appears to be some relationship between the timing of the introduction of legislation and an improvement in the relative position of women in the labor market with respect to pay. However, examination of pay movements in other European countries suggests no such correspondence, though the relative position of women appears to have improved in these countries also. Since this general improvement contrasts with experience in the United States, which has a more extensive legislative framework than any of the European countries, it seems worthwhile to examine how far one can derive conclusions relevant to U.S. policy in this area.

THE CHANGING PAY STRUCTURE

The Overall Earnings Differential in Britain

Prior to the introduction of the Equal Pay Act in 1970 the male/female earnings differential in Britain was remarkably constant. For full-time adult manual workers, female/male average weekly earnings varied only between 49 and 52 percent over the period 1955 to 1970, while for average hourly earnings the figure was even more

Table 14-1. Gross Weekly Earnings Sex Differential in Great Britain.

| Year (April) | Female Earnings as a Percentage of Male 1970–83, All Industries and Services | | |
	Nonmanual Workers	Manual Workers	All Workers
1970	49.7	50.0	54.3
1971	50.6	52.0	55.6
1972	51.0	52.1	55.9
1973	51.4	51.7	55.1
1974	52.6	54.1	56.4
1975	57.9	57.6	61.5
1976	59.8	60.5	64.3
1977	60.5	61.1	64.9
1978	58.7	61.2	63.3
1979	58.4	59.4	62.1
1980	58.5	60.9	63.3
1981	59.3	61.1	65.1
1982	58.6	59.9	64.1
1983	59.1	61.2	65.0

Source: *New Earnings Surveys* 1970–83. Figures relate to those workers not affected by absence; full-time men age 21 and over and full-time women age 18 and over.

stable—between 60 and 62 percent over the period 1950–70 (Office of Manpower Economics 1972: 10–11).

Table 14-1 provides New Earnings Survey data on the movement in the gross weekly earnings differential from 1970–1983 for adult workers whose pay was not affected by absence. In contrast to the earlier period, the position of females improved by 10.7 percentage points but the major improvement (7.9 percentage points) was experienced in 1975 and 1976. It should be noted that the 1970 Equal Pay Act was introduced on a gradual basis, only becoming fully effective in 1975, and the Sex Discrimination Act was also passed in that same year. Thus, this improvement coincided with legislative changes.

In one sense the sex differential figure for all workers gives a misleading impression. While the ratio for 1983 was 65 percent for all workers, for manual workers it was only 61.2 percent and for nonmanual workers only 59.1 percent. This paradox is explained by the fact that the differential is more favorable to women in the manual

Table 14-2. Male/Female Earnings Differential and Relative Employment in Great Britain, 1970–83.

Year (April)	Nonmanual Workers		Manual Workers		All Workers	
	Female Employment[a] as Percentage of Male	Female Earnings[b] as Percentage of Male	Female Employment as Percentage of Male	Female Earnings as Percentage of Male	Female Employment as Percentage of Male	Female Earnings as Percentage of Male
1970	73.9	52.5	21.3	61.7	40.4	63.7
1971	73.2	53.2	21.2	61.3	40.1	63.3
1972	74.5	54.0	21.4	61.8	40.9	64.0
1973	74.2	54.3	21.5	62.0	41.4	63.7
1974	73.3	55.5	21.4	64.4	41.0	65.1
1975	72.5	60.7	19.6	68.0	40.9	69.9
1976	74.9	62.6	20.0	71.1	42.3	72.6
1977	76.4	63.1	20.6	71.7	43.5	72.9
1978	76.0	61.2	21.0	72.0	44.0	71.3
1979	77.7	61.0	20.8	70.2	44.6	70.5
1980	77.6	61.1	21.2	70.9	45.6	71.8
1981	78.8	61.8	20.2	69.9	46.7	72.8
1982	80.0	61.0	20.9	68.8	47.9	71.9
1983	80.3	61.4	21.2	69.6	48.8	72.2

a. Employment refers to all full-time adults in the sample (that is, males age 21 and over and females age 18 and over) whose pay for the survey period was unaffected by absence.

b. Earnings are average gross hourly earnings excluding overtime pay and overtime hours of those adults whose pay was not affected by absence.

Source: *New Earnings Surveys 1970–83.*

sector but that the majority of women (unlike men) are engaged in nonmanual work, where average earnings are higher for women as well as for men.

We must allow, also, for the fact that men work longer hours than women, though it is difficult to determine how far this difference reflects either preferences on the part of employees or opportunities offered by employers. Notwithstanding this, in 1983 men worked an average of 41.5 hours compared to 37.2 hours for women. Table 14-2 allows for this by providing figures for average gross hourly earnings excluding overtime pay and overtime hours for those adults whose pay was not affected by absence. This has the effect of raising relative female pay by two or three percentage points for nonmanual workers and ten or eleven percentage points for manual workers.

It is clear from Table 14-2 that the improvement in relative female earnings ceased in 1977 or 1978 and the ratio subsequently stabilized at a slightly lower level. Yet this improvement in female relative pay has not been accompanied by a decline in female relative employment opportunities, since female employment as a proportion of male has grown over the whole period in the case of nonmanual workers and has been remarkably stable in the case of manual workers. It is not wholly clear to what extent this reflects the growth of employment opportunities in traditional female jobs, though the development of service employment and the demise of manufacturing points in this direction. However, we need to allow for variations in hours worked by men and women. Zabalza and Tzannatos (1983) show that although the total number of hours worked by women increased by 17.6 percent relative to those of men between 1970 and 1980 there was a slowdown in the annual growth rate from 2.7 percent during 1970-75 to 0.6 percent during 1975-80. Further, a substantial part of this increase in female employment was found in the public sector. In the private sector relative employment grew only by 1.9 percent over the period 1970-75 and fell by 0.4 percent per annum during the period 1975-80. Nevertheless, they conclude that this fall is not as large as one might expect.

The Components of Pay

Overtime and shiftwork attract premium rates of pay for the vast majority of workers and can make a significant impact on weekly earnings. Similarly workers are able to increase earnings directly in return for greater effort where payment-by-results methods are utilized. These three components amounted to 14.6 percent of weekly earnings for males compared to 5.8 percent for women in 1983, averaged out among all full-time workers regardless of whether they received such payments or not. This overall figure conceals substantial differences between manual and nonmanual workers with regard to the receipt of such payments. Thus manual men received 24.0 percent of their weekly income from these sources compared to 14.3 percent in the case of manual women, but the corresponding figure for nonmanual men was only 6.7 percent and for nonmanual women only 3.8 percent. In general we can say that men's earnings are increased relative to those of women by two factors: Relatively more men receive such payments, and the size of such payments is generally larger for men. Nonetheless, substantial earnings differences remain after these additional components of pay have been eliminated.

In this context it should be noted that the conditions of employment of women are limited by legislation, the most notable of which are the Factories Act 1961 and the Employment of Women and Young Persons Act 1963. Limits operate on the maximum daily and weekly working hours, maximum continuous spell of work, earliest starting and latest finishing times, and the length and timing of overtime work. With certain exceptions restrictions also apply to female employment in factories on night shifts, on Sundays, and on other public holidays, though exemption orders can be and are sought from the Health and Safety Executive.

The Occupational Differential

It is instructive to examine how far these general trends have been reflected at levels disaggregated by occupation, industry, or (public/private) sector. There are some occupations in which women do relatively much better compared to men than the general rule and others where they fare considerably worse. Thus in 1983 female hourly earnings reached 94.6 percent of those for males in security and protective services, but the relevant figure in selling was only 56.6 percent. All occupations show an improvement in female relative pay, but the timing differs with the date when the highest female/male

earnings ratio was attained, varying between 1977 and 1983 depending on the occupation. There is much less occupational conformity,
therefore, than might be inferred from the global figures.

The Industrial Differential

These findings are confirmed in the earnings by industry results.
Nonmanual women fare best relative to men in miscellaneous services
where the earnings ratio was 70.6 in 1983 and worst in insurance,
banking finance, and business services where the ratio was only 52.2
in 1983. Manual women fared best in transport and communication
(84.4 percent) and worst in paper, printing, and publishing (62.9
percent). There appears to be little correspondence between the relative position of nonmanual women and that of manual women by
industry. This is confirmed by the peak years for the earnings ratio
in industries where sufficiently long runs of data are available, which
varies between 1976 and 1982.[1] Again, therefore, there is much less
uniformity by industry than might be suggested by aggregate figures.
We cannot infer that this necessarily means that the implementation
of the legislation varied in timing among industries, since the aggregate earnings in each industry will alter with changes in the composition of the labor force and the published New Earnings Survey data
do not enable us to cross-tabulate separately for occupation by
industry.

The Public/Private Sector Differential

We might expect that there would be greater pressure on public sector employers to conform with the requirements of equal pay and
opportunities legislation than is generally the case for private sector
employers. The data in Table 14-3 show that for all workers the sex
differential has been consistently narrower in the public sector, but
it is the private sector in which the more substantial improvement
in female pay has occurred (a gain of 11.2 percentage points over the
period 1970-83, compared to a gain of only 4.7 percentage points
in the public sector). This, doubtless reflects the fact that equal pay
for broadly comparable work was already the norm in the public
sector prior to the introduction of legislation. Again there are strik-

Table 14-3. Gross Weekly Earnings Sex Differential in the Public and Private Sectors in Great Britain.

| | Female Earnings as a Percentage of Male, 1970–83 | | | | | |
| | Nonmanual Workers | | Manual Workers | | All Workers | |
	Public Sector	Private Sector	Public Sector	Private Sector	Public Sector	Private Sector
1970	59.5	43.4	52.4	48.9	65.9	48.1
1974	59.8	46.6	58.5	52.8	65.4	51.4
1975	65.1	49.8	61.1	56.7	69.4	54.7
1976	66.6	51.3	63.2	59.6	72.1	56.8
1977	67.3	52.4	63.1	60.4	72.0	57.8
1978	65.9	51.4	62.2	60.9	70.3	57.6
1979	65.6	51.6	59.2	59.4	68.9	56.9
1980	64.9	51.9	62.3	60.4	69.3	57.8
1981	65.4	52.9	61.8	61.1	71.3	59.1
1982	64.3	52.7	60.1	60.0	69.7	58.8
1983	65.3	52.6	61.7	61.1	70.6	59.3

Source: *New Earnings Surveys* 1970–83. Figures relate to those workers not affected by absence, full-time men age 21 and over and full-time women age 18 and over.

ing differences between the relative positions of nonmanual and manual workers. For nonmanual workers a substantial difference in the sex ratio remained in 1983, with the public sector ratio being some 12.7 percentage points above that pertaining in the private sector, but the gap between public and private sector differentials had been virtually eliminated for manual workers by 1983.

Earnings and Education

There are many other variables that will impinge on the sex earnings differential, but we are predominantly concerned with changes in the ratio over time, and some of the variables that are important in the cross-section may well be fairly stable as far as time series analyses are concerned.

The level of education received prior to entry into the labor market and the amount and nature of on- or off-the-job training received thereafter have been shown to have a substantial effect on earnings,[2] but the crucial question here is whether increasing opportunities for women in education and training have contributed to the narrowing of the sex differential.

Examining attainment in school General Certificate of Education examinations girls obtained roughly 50 percent of all passes throughout the period 1970–80, but this proportion varies substantially by discipline from 3.1 percent in technical drawing to 98.1 percent in cookery in 1980. There is a tendency for the degree of segregation in passes in particular subjects to reduce over time. For example, the female proportion of passes in mathematics rose from 37.5 percent in 1970 to 42.1 percent in 1980. Similar trends can be detected in the advanced level passes, but, in addition, here the overall female proportion of passes is increasing—from 40.4 percent in 1970 to 45.0 percent in 1980. In the universities too the proportion of female students has shown a steady increase at both undergraduate and postgraduate levels, but again, there are wide variations by discipline, from 6.9 percent in engineering and technology to 67.8 percent in language, literature, and area studies in 1980, and the gap in male-dominated disciplines is narrowing slowly.

The above differences by sex are repeated for those who leave the educational system in terms of opportunities for training. In 1981 women represented only 18.4 percent of all young persons ages 16 to 18 released by their employers during working hours for part-time study. Women represent a much higher proportion of those on the Training Opportunities Programme, but women on such courses are heavily concentrated in shorthand, typing, and clerical courses that have been cut back most severely in the recession. In general, it would seem that the relative improvement in the relative educational profile of women has not been rapid enough to explain a substantial part of the improvement in the relative earnings of women. It takes many years for a change in the inflow of educated manpower to have an appreciable effect on the stock of educated manpower.

The Effect of Trade Union Organisation

In theory trade unions could either narrow the sex earnings differential by obtaining a higher mark up for women than for men or widen it by excluding women disproportionately to men from the benefits of unionization. Women have a lower propensity to join trade unions than do men, but in recent years they have been entering union membership faster than have men. While in 1970 females comprised 24.5 percent of total union membership, by 1981 the figure had reached 31 percent. In absolute terms female unionization peaked in 1979, but the loss of union members in the recession following that year has been slightly higher proportionately for men. An analysis by Nickell (1977), using 1973 collective bargaining coverage data, found that the union wage effect was slightly greater for women than for men (19 percent as opposed to 18 percent). Given the disparity in union membership between the sexes, it seems clear, however, that the net effect of unions in Britain has been to widen the gross male/female earnings differential.

The Effects of Recession

The 1970s and early 1980s saw in Britain, as in other countries, rising unemployment. It can be hypothesized that the gross earnings differential between males and females will be related to the state of the labor market and more specifically that such differentials will widen during recessions and narrow during buoyant economic conditions. The reason for this is that during recessions access to jobs will become more difficult, particularly so for women, since given discriminatory tastes on the part of the employer, potential demand can be met simply by hiring men for preferred jobs, using sex as a screening device to the exclusion of women. In tight labor markets, in contrast, labor shortages may force employers to hire women even in what have traditionally been male jobs. Furthermore, the effect of tight labor markets will be to eliminate the excess supply of unskilled workers, while part of the excess demand for skilled workers can be met by upgrading. Consequently the skill differential tends to narrow at the peak of the cycle and to widen at the trough. Since women are unskilled to a disproportionate extent relative to men, the male/female earnings differential may be expected to narrow during periods of high activity and widen during periods of low activity for this reason.

Yet a regression analysis of the female hourly earnings ratio in Britain over the period 1950–80 reveals no relationship between the dependent variable and cyclical indicators (the change in real GNP at factor cost and lagged unemployment) (Jain and Sloane 1983a, 1983b). Possible explanations are that the lowest-paid women are driven out of employment which raises the average pay for those women who remain in employment, that men suffer disproportionately from reduced overtime earnings, or that women are protected by their predominance in service jobs.

THE IMPACT OF LEGISLATION IN BRITAIN AND EUROPE

The Legislative Framework

The United Kingdom was the first of the current members of the European Community to introduce equal pay legislation. The 1970 Equal Pay Act was unusual in two respects. First, there was a transition period for implementation so that full equality did not have to be granted until the end of 1975. This was to allow for the fact that the costs of implementation would vary considerably among employers according to the number of men and women employed for whom a valid comparison could be made. Second, the act represented a half-way house between the concept of equal pay for equal work and equal pay for work of equal value. The act states that men and women should be paid at the same rate if they are either employed on the same or broadly similar work or where the jobs of men and women have been rated as equivalent under a job evaluation scheme. For a job to qualify as "broadly similar" differences between activities that men undertake and those that women undertake should not be of practical importance—in frequency as well as nature. There is no compulsion under the 1970 act to introduce job evaluation, but where it is used it must not be weighted unfairly in favor of one sex or other nor may one group be paid more than another where they are rated as equal under such a scheme.

As a member of the European Community U.K. law is now subject to Community Law. Article 119 of the Treaty of Rome lays down the principle of equal pay for equal work, but in 1975 a council directive interpreted the principle to apply to equal pay for work of equal value (Commission of the European Communities 1980: 19). This directive required member states to introduce legislation within one year, to ban legal or administrative measures in conflict with the principle of equal pay, and to ensure equality of treatment for men and women in relation to pay in collective agreements and individual employment contracts. The commission noted that the national laws of some member states were not in conformity with the new Community norms and instituted infringement procedures against seven members in March 1977.[3] In the European Court of Justice it was argued that the United Kingdom had failed to give full effect to the provisions of article 119, and the equal pay directive, because there was no provision in the 1970 act for equal pay for work of equal value unless a job evaluation scheme had been carried out. Furthermore, there was no obligation on the employer to carry out such an evaluation, and where it had been carried out, the U.K. courts had held it not to be binding unless accepted by both parties. Finally, it was not possible to challenge hidden or indirect discrimination under the 1970 act. The Court found in favor of the Commission in July 1982, and consequently the government introduced the Equal Pay (Amendment) Regulation 1983, which became operative on 1 January 1984 (Landau 1984). Under these regulations a tribunal may commission a report from an independent expert, appointed from a list of experts designated by the Advisory, Conciliation, and Arbitration Service (ACAS), to consider whether work is of equal value in cases where there is no formal job evaluation scheme. The expert has to assess job content, which itself is a form of job evaluation (McCrudden 1983). It remains to be seen to what extent this alteration in the legislation will influence the male/female earnings differential.[4]

Aggrieved individuals may be assisted by the Equal Opportunities Commission (EOC). In addition this body has strategic functions, being empowered to investigate an employer's or industry's employment practices, to issue nondiscrimination notices, and to demand that relevant information be produced. Most complaints are, however, settled at the conciliation stage through the intervention of ACAS. It is important to note that in Britain the emphasis is on individual complaint; there is nothing equivalent to the U.S. emphasis on systemwide enforcement through such devices as pattern or practice and class-action court suits.[5] In the European Community only Ireland has the equivalent of the EOC, but Denmark, France, and Italy are presently setting up equality councils along the lines of the British model.

Table 14–4. Discrimination Applications, Great Britain.

	Equal Pay				Sex Discrimination			
	Number of Applications	Percentage Settled by Conciliation and/or Withdrawn	Percentage Upheld by Tribunal	Percentage Dismissed by Tribunal	Number of Applications	Percentage Settled by Conciliation and/or Withdrawn	Percentage Upheld by Tribunal	Percentage Dismissed by Tribunal
1976	1,742	59.3	12.2	28.5	243	51.0	9.9	39.1
1977	751	51.7	12.1	26.2	229	66.4	7.4	26.2
1978	343	76.7	7.0	16.3	171	60.8	8.2	31.0
1979	263	70.3	4.9	24.8	178	66.1	8.9	25.0
1980	91	71.4	4.4	24.2	180	61.3	8.3	30.4
1981	54	50.0	11.1	29.9	256	64.5	7.3	28.2
1982	39	67.0	5.0	28.0	150	62.7	16.0	21.3

Source: *Employment Gazette.* London: Her Majesty's Stationery Office. Compiled from various monthly issues.

Use of the Legislation in Britain

The extent to which employees have made use of the legislation in Britain is small and dwindling. As Table 14-4 illustrates, the number of applications under the Equal Pay Act has fallen from 1,742 in 1976 to a mere 39 in 1982, while the corresponding figures under the Sex Discrimination Act are 243 and 150. This does not represent an aversion to the use of legislation on the part of the British workforce: There are, for example, nearly 30,000 unfair dismissal cases each year. Perhaps there is a lack of knowledge concerning the rights of individuals. Certainly this appears to be the case with employers among whom the EOC has detected massive ignorance of the details of the legislation (EOC 1979). Another factor might be the *positive* knowledge that prospects of a successful outcome for the individual are rather low relative to other forms of employee protection legislation.

As Table 14-4 illustrates, out of the approximately one-third of applications that are not settled by conciliation or withdrawn the probability of the case being upheld by a tribunal is much lower than the probability of its dismissal. Employees may also have been influenced by an awareness of the depressed state of the labor market and their fear of retaliation by the employer—a view expressed by the EOC in its 1982 report (EOC 1983: 1). On the employers' side we might conclude that the probability of being taken to court is rather low, which may explain in part why the employment of women has stayed up so well subsequent to the introduction of the legislation.

Assessing the Impact of British Equal
Opportunities Legislation

The first attempt to test for the effect of the British legislation on the male/female earnings differential was that of Chiplin, Curran, and Parsley (Sloane 1980: ch. 3). They estimated an equation for the differential during the period prior to the passing of the act in order to predict what might have occurred in the absence of legislation. They found, unlike earlier results for the United States, that relative earnings did not improve as labor markets tightened, that female relative earnings were, ceteris paribus, worsening over time (the time trend being negative), and that in 1975 the female/male earnings ratio was some 8 percent higher than it would have been but for a change in the underlying relationship. However, it appeared that the influence of flat-rate incomes policies had been stronger than equal pay and opportunities legislation in achieving this result.[6]

This latter suggestion has recently been challenged by Zabalza and Tzannatos (1983), who include an incomes policy variable directly in their model.[7] In their two-stage least-squares estimates for 1950–80, all the included variables—apart from the cyclical indicator, which does not have the expected sign—are significant. The results suggest that the overall effect of the legislation has been to increase the relative earnings of women by 18.8 percent, if the nonsignificant effect of 1972 is taken into account, or by 17.3 percent if that effect is ignored. In practice, the increase in relative female employment has reduced this gain to 14.8 percent. The effect of incomes policy on the other hand is only 1.7 percent.[8]

There is reason, however, to treat these estimates with a degree of caution. First, Zabalza and Tzannatos's incomes policies dummies do not appear to conform to those periods that are most clearly equalizing. Second, the New Earnings Survey taken in one week in April does not tell us when the annual pay adjustment takes place for each bargaining unit. Ideally we require a continuous earnings series. Third, standard dummies do not enable us to account fully for incomes policies of varying degrees of equalization. Fourth, there is a degree of overlapping of the incomes policy and equal pay dummies with the time trend, which itself could be picking up some of these effects and which may give rise to problems of multicolinearity (r varies between 0.68 and 0.81 for T and the equal pay dummies). It is also worth pointing out that the period when female relative pay improved markedly was one of unprecedented inflation. For example, between April 1974 and April 1975 the index of average earnings rose by 30.7 percent. From an employer's perspective the cost of raising female relative pay might have appeared slight in relation to the general upward movement in pay. Perhaps it is safest simply to say that Britain coincidently chose to combine equal pay legislation with flat-rate incomes policies and together these raised relative female pay. How successful the one would have been without the other is a matter for conjecture.

A final question to ask is how does this improvement in female relative pay compare with what one might reasonably expect. Using a human capital model, studies by Greenhalgh (1980) and Siebert and Sloane (1981), concentrating on nonmarried workers, have found sex discrimination in earnings (not dissimilar to comparable analyses for the United States) in the order of 10 percent—that is, women earn 10 percent less than men simply because they are women. Since this represents only roughly one-quarter of the total difference in earnings between men and women, it might not be unreasonable to suggest that a further improvement in the relative position of women is likely to depend more on changes in attitudes toward family and labor market roles than on further adjustments in equality of opportunity legislation. Further support for this view is found in a recent analysis of wage differentials between married men and married women by Zabalza and Arrufat (1983), who find that equality legislation has achieved between one-half and three-quarters of the total gains required to eliminate discrimination.

The Experience in Other European Countries

It seems highly appropriate to consider the earnings differential in other member countries of the European Community, given the increasing role that the European legislative framework is playing in this as in other areas of employment. The Eurostat publication, *Hourly Earnings/Hours of Work*, gives data on gross hourly earnings from 1964 for the original six members of the community and from 1975 for the remaining four current members. The main data are limited to hourly earnings including overtime and to manual employees in manufacturing industries, but if these countries follow the British pattern, there should be some correspondence between the behavior of the differential for earnings including overtime and those net of overtime and between that for manual workers and for nonmanual workers.[9] Table 14-5 shows that the female/male earnings differential improved in each of the six countries, but at markedly different rates between 1964 and 1968—with France (3.0 percent), Germany (5.5 percent), and Belgium (9.2 percent) showing much less change than Italy (23.4 percent), Netherlands (26.7 percent), and Luxembourg (31.1 percent). In all countries other than Luxembourg the gap is narrower at the end of the period than in Britain, with Italy having the narrowest gap of all at 13.9 percent. In Germany growth has been slow but even; in France there was a sharp increase

Table 14-5. Gross Hourly Earnings Differential in Various Countries of the European Community.

Manual Workers, Total Manufacturing Industries 1964–82,
Female Earnings as a Percentage of Male

	Germany	France	Italy	Netherlands	Belgium	Luxembourg	Britain	United States[b]
1964	68.8	76.0	69.8	55.0	65.3	45.3	—	60
1968	—	—	73.7	59.7	—	—	—	58
1969	69.4	77.4	72.8	60.7	68.0	53.7	—	61
1970	70.0	76.4	71.0	60.8	68.1	51.9	—	59
1971	69.9	76.3	76.4	60.6	67.9	56.4	—	60
1972	70.2	76.0	76.8	62.1	68.8	57.8	59.5[a]	58
1973	70.0	80.1	75.2	66.4	68.1	55.5	59.8	57
1974	70.8	75.9	77.5	69.0	69.2	57.1	62.4	59
1975	72.0	76.1	80.3	72.5	71.1	59.9	66.1	59
1976	72.1	75.8	80.1	74.5	71.6	64.0	68.8	60
1977	72.1	75.5	84.3	74.8	71.1	61.4	70.3	59
1978	72.7	75.5	85.2	75.2	70.9	58.7	69.4	59
1979	72.3	75.9	86.4	75.3	70.9	56.0	69.5	60
1980	72.3	77.3	86.1	74.8	70.4	58.0	70.3	60
1981	72.9	77.4	85.5	75.3	71.4	60.5	69.1	60
1982	72.8	78.3	86.1	75.2	71.9	59.4	68.9	NA

a. This figure relates to October rather than April of this year.

b. Source: *Current Population Survey 1964–81*—Annual Earnings of Full-time Year-round Wage and Salary Workers. These are not on a comparable basis to the figures for the European countries.

Source: Eurostat, *"Hourly Earnings—Hours of Work,"* 1975–82.

Note: Figures relate to April and include bonuses, overtime earnings, and so forth.

in 1973 followed by an equally sharp decline; in Italy the improvement came in the mid-1960s, 1971, 1975, and 1977; in the Netherlands in the mid-1960s and 1972 to 1976; in Belgium there has been no real change since 1975; and in Luxembourg most of the improvement occurred between 1964 and 1972. There is no clear pattern, therefore, in these countries, nor does the timing match that in Britain.

How far then do these adjustments match legislative changes in each of these countries? In Germany equality of opportunity legislation encompassing the principle of equality between men and women in placement, working conditions, and occupational advancement was adopted by Parliament only in 1980, though certain protection was offered by article 3 of the Basic Law on Equality of the Citizens 1949. In France an equal pay act was passed in 1972 and implemented through directive in 1973, and equal opportunity acts followed in 1975 covering discrimination in hiring or firing because of sex and race and in 1983 including equal pay for work of equal value and extending equality to family situations. The timing of the former corresponds to the upward adjustment in the earnings rates observed in 1973, but that gain was immediately lost in the subsequent year. In Italy an antidiscrimination act covering both equal pay and equal opportunity was passed in 1977, but here the rapid improvement in female relative pay clearly preceded the introduction of legislation. Likewise most of the improvement in female relative earnings in the Netherlands had occurred before the equal pay act was passed in 1975, but further equal opportunity legislation was introduced in 1980. In Belgium the whole of the improvement occurred before equal pay was concluded through collective agreement in 1975 (the National Employment Council's Collective Labour Agreement No. 25, rendered mandatory by Royal Decree in December of that year), with equality of opportunity legislation following in 1978. Finally Luxembourg introduced equal pay legislation in 1974 after the improvement in female relative earnings had largely been concluded, with equal opportunities legislation following in December 1981. The evidence, therefore, appears to be overwhelming: Far from being responsible for improvements in female relative earnings, legislation has tended to follow them.

This conclusion is hardly altered when reference is made to the remaining European Community countries for which data are available on a comparable basis to the above from October 1975. Ireland tends to follow Britain in terms of labor legislation and passed an Antidiscrimination (Pay) Act in 1974 and an Employment Equality Act in 1977. Here female relative earnings stood at 60.9 percent of male in October 1975 and 68.4 percent in April 1982, the improvement being concentrated in the late 1970s.[10] Denmark passed an Equal Pay Law in 1976 and an Equal Treatment Act in 1978, but female relative earnings hardly changed between October 1975 (84.3 percent) and April 1982 (85.1 percent). In Greece equal pay was granted under article 22 of the 1975 constitution, and equal treatment legislation took effect at the beginning of 1984, though applying essentially only to the private sector and the self-employed. Here female relative earnings stood at 69.9 percent of male in October 1975 and rose to 73.2 percent in April 1982.

As far as non-European Community countries are concerned Sweden is another example of the above phenomenon. Here the female earnings ratio rose from 78 percent in 1968 to 87 percent in 1977, antidiscrimination legislation following in 1978. In Norway the ratio rose from 75 percent in 1968 to 80 percent in 1977, and equal pay legislation followed in 1978. In Austria the ratio rose from 67 percent in 1960 to 74 percent in 1977, while equal pay legislation was introduced in 1979. Finally there is the example of the United States, which has the most extensive equal pay and opportunities legislation but a female earnings ratio that has been remarkably constant over time and significantly lower than in the majority of OECD countries. Overall, then, the evidence strongly supports the view that legislation is neither a necessary nor a sufficient condition for the attainment of equality between the sexes.

CONCLUSIONS

In many respects the relative position of women in Britain has been similar to that facing women in the United States. Until the 1970s the ratio of female to male earnings was very close in the two countries (in the order of 60 percent or so), and female labor force participation has also been of similar magnitude and has increased at approximately the same rate. The United States preceded Britain in introducing equal pay and opportunities legislation and associated administrative apparatus and also has gone further in utilizing an affirmative action framework and extensive legal penalties for those who infringe the law. Yet in the mid-1970s it was in Britain that the relative position of women began to improve with regard to earnings, while in the United States the sex/wage differential remained fixed as if through some divine law. Econometric analyses point to the influence of legislation in effecting change in Britain, though the precise role of incomes policy in assisting in this improvement is still a matter of dispute. Evidence from the rest of the EEC and elsewhere does suggest on the other hand that it is possible for the relative position of women to improve without legislation and that the introduction of legislation is no guarantee of effecting improvement. Despite this the European Community is pressing member states to implement fully the various Community directives on equal treatment for men and women.[11] It seems clear that further progress in the relative position of women will require fundamental changes in social attitudes and behavior outside the labor market.

NOTES

1. The only industry for which relative female pay was not significantly higher at the end of the period than the start was public administration (for nonmanual workers only). Tzannatos and Zabalza (1983) suggest that this is consistent with the fact that for the majority of workers in this sector (most of whom are white-collar) the principle of equal pay was already in operation at the beginning of the period.

2. See, for example, Greenhalgh (1980) for a cross-section analysis using data from the 1975 *General Household Survey* (Office of Population Censuses and Surveys 1975).

3. The countries concerned were Belgium, Denmark, France, Germany, Luxembourg, the Netherlands, and the United Kingdom.

4. Both the House of Lords and the EOC have argued that this amendment to the Equal Pay Act does not go far enough in order to meet the requirements of the European Directive.

5. Equality of opportunity in Britain is covered by the Sex Discrimination Act of 1975, which prohibits discrimination on grounds of gender or marriage with respect to hiring, opportunities for promotion, transfer and training, and dismissal procedures. An unusual feature of the British legislation is that the act offers protection to married persons of either sex, to single men and women separately, but not to single persons as a group. In addition to direct discrimination, where a woman is treated less favorably than a man simply because she is a woman, there is also provision for indirect discrimination. Mirroring developments in the United States this

occurs where a requirement or condition is applied equally to men and to women but is such that (a) the proportion of women who can comply with it is smaller than is the case for men, (b) the employer cannot demonstrate it to be justifiable irrespective of the sex of the person to whom it is applied, and (c) it is to the detriment of the woman concerned. Unlike the U.S. legislation there are in general no provisions for affirmative action. One exception is that the act permits special access to training facilities for one sex only where, within the previous twelve months, there were no or very few persons of that sex performing the work in question. Under the U.K. legislation the individual has the right to take his or her case to an industrial tribunal, with right of appeal to the Employment Appeals Tribunal and ultimately the House of Lords or the European Court of Justice. The initial burden of proof is on the complainant to show the existence of a particular requirement and that the requirement operated to his or her detriment. If this is accepted, the burden of proof transfers to the employer to demonstrate that the requirement is justified.

In February 1976 the Council of Europe promulgated an Equal Treatment Directive that defined equal treatment as "all discrimination on the ·grounds of sex either directly or indirectly by reference in particular to marital or family status." There are certain exceptions where sex is a genuine occupational qualification, for pregnancy and maternity, and where measures to promote equal opportunity for women (by removing existing inequalities) are required. The question of age of retirement is not so far covered by Community law. The British legislation—excluding as it does discrimination against single persons and making no reference to family status—may not meet fully the requirements of European law.

6. Using admittedly crude assumptions about the impact of flat-rate incomes policies, only two percentage points would be left to be explained by the equality legislation. However, Chiplin et al. (1980) end their analysis period in 1975, and there was a further substantial upward shift in the female/male differential in 1976.

7. Their demand equation is:

$$\ln(WF/WM) = \alpha_0 + \alpha_1 \ln(FH/MH) + \alpha_2 \ln(I) + \alpha_3 \ln(Q/Q^*)$$
$$+ \alpha_4 T + \alpha_5 D + \alpha_6 IP + \epsilon$$

where

(FH/MH) = women's hours relative to male hours

I = industrial structure index to allow for the possibility that sectors that have expanded more are more intensive in the employment of women (achieved by holding constant the distribution of male employment over the period)

(Q/Q^*) = relative deviation of $GNP(Q)$ from a linear trend (Q^*)

T = time trend to allow for differing productivity (changes in education) between men and women

D = legislation dummies taking the value of 0 prior to 1971 and one thereafter for 1971, 1972, 1974, and 1975

IP = incomes policies dummies with values of 1 for 1973 and 1976–78.

8. If we ignored compositional effects and assumed that the erosion of the differential since the peak up to 1983 was entirely due to the temporary effect of incomes policy, the implied effects of income policies would be 1.7 percentage points for nonmanual workers and 2.4 percentage points for manual workers. This represents 16 percent of the change in the differential from 1970 to the peak for the former and 23.3 percent for the latter.

9. In fact, the Eurostat publication does provide indexes of gross hourly earnings of nonmanual workers in manufacturing industries with October 1972 equal to 100, which confirm the latter proposition. In October 1981 the indexes were as follows:

	Men	Women
Germany	143.7	148.1
France	195.4	205.9
Italy	269.6	297.8
Netherlands	148.4	155.3
Belgium	162.0	165.8
Luxembourg	161.8	164.3

10. Data from another source show that the average hourly earnings ratio in nonagricultural industries had already risen in Ireland from 55 percent in 1968 to 61 percent in 1973 (OECD 1980: 32).

11. See EEC equality action program 1982–85, suggesting a whole range of initiatives.

REFERENCES

Chiplin, B., Curran, M. M., and Parsley, C. J. 1980. "Relative Female Earnings in Great Britain and the Impact of Legislation." In *Women and Low Pay*, pp. 57–126. Edited by P. J. Sloane. New York: MacMillan.

Commission of the European Communities. 1980. *Women and the European Community: Community Actions and Comparative National Situations.* Brussels: Commission of the European Communities.

European Economic Community. 1982–85. *Equality Action Program.* Brussels: Commission of the European Communities.

Equal Opportunities Commission (EOC). 1979. *Third Annual Report: 1978.* Manchester, England: H.M.S.O.

_____. 1983. *Seventh Annual Report: 1982.* Manchester, England: H.M.S.O.

Greenhalgh, C. 1980. "Male-Female Wage Differentials in Great Britain: Is Marriage an Equal Opportunity?" *Economic Journal* 90(360) (December): 751–75.

Jain, H.C., and P.J. Sloane. 1983a. "The Challenge of Unemployment to Equal Opportunities in the U.S.A., Canada and Britain." *Proceedings of the Sixth World Congress of the International Industrial Relations Association.* Kyoto, Japan, March 28–31.

_____. 1983b. "The Impact of Recession on Equal Opportunities for Minorities and Women in the United States, Canada and Britain." *Columbia Journal of World Business* 18(2) (Summer): 16–27.

Landau, C.E. 1984. "Recent Legislation and Case Law in the EEC on Sex Equality in Employment." *International Labour Review* 123(1) (January/February): 53–70.

McCrudden, Christopher. 1983. "Equal Pay for Work of Equal Value: The Equal Pay (Amendment) Regulations 1983." *Industrial Law Journal* 12(4) (December): 197–219.

Nickell, S. 1977. "Trade Unions and the Position of Women in the Industrial Wages Structure." *British Journal of Industrial Relations* 15(2) (July): 192–210.

OECD. 1980. *Women and Employment: Policies for Equal Opportunities.* Paris: OECD.

Office of Manpower Economics. 1972. *Equal Pay: First Report by the Office of Manpower Economics.* London: H.M.S.O.

Office of Population Censuses and Surveys. 1975. *General Household Survey.* London: Office of Population Censuses and Surveys.

Siebert, W.S., and P.J. Sloane. 1981. "The Measurement of Sex and Marital Status Discrimination at the Workplace." *Economica* 48 (May): 125–41.

Tzannatos, P.Z., and A. Zabalza. 1983. "The Anatomy of the Rise of British Relative Wages in the 1970s: Evidence from the New Earnings Survey." Discussion Paper 157. London: Centre for Labour Economics, London School of Economics.

Zabalza, A., and J. Arrufat. 1983. "Wage Differentials between Married Men and Women in Great Britain: The Depreciation Effect on Non-Participation." Discussion Paper 151. London: Centre for Labour Economics, London School of Economics.

Zabalza, A., and Z. Tzannatos. 1983. "The Effects of Britain's Anti-discriminatory Legislation on Relative Pay and Employment." Discussion Paper 155. London: Centre for Labour Economics, London School of Economics.

15 WAGE DISCRIMINATION
A Family Issue

Winn Newman
Christine L. Owens

The disastrous impact of sex-based wage discrimination on the U.S. family is increasing as more and more women enter the workforce[1] and contribute in whole or in part to the support of their families.[2] Between 1970 and 1983 the number of two-parent families dropped 5 percent, while at the same time the number of single-parent families doubled (U.S. Department of Labor, Women's Bureau 1984: 1). Ninety percent of these single-parent families were maintained by women (U.S. Department of Labor 1984: 4).

Women and children constitute the largest discrete component of "the poor" in this country. Women head nearly half of all the poor U.S. families; within the black community nearly 72 percent of all families below the poverty level are maintained by women (U.S. Department of Labor, Women's Bureau 1984: 3).

A major reason for poverty among women is the limited opportunity available to them in the labor market (Pearce and McAdoo 1981).[3] Access to employment, however, does not rid women and their families of the effects of poverty[4] because even when they find work, the wages that women earn are severely depressed. At every level of educational achievement, for example, women are paid substantially less than men. Consider that, although men and women

The authors wish to express their appreciation to Nancy Sachitano for her fine work on this article.

workers are almost equally educated (12.8 and 12.7 years of school, respectively), women are paid only 63 cents on every dollar that men earn (U.S. Department of Labor, Women's Bureau 1984: 3). Women workers with four or more years of college are paid only slightly more than men with one to three years of high school, and women with high school educations are paid less than men who have completed less than eight years of elementary school.[5]

The primary cause of these wage differentials is sex-based wage discrimination—that is, paying women less for the work they do simply because they are women. Sex-based wage discrimination thus contributes directly to the incidence of poverty among women and children in this country. If working women, particularly working mothers, were paid wages commensurate with those of similarly qualified men, *half of the families now living in poverty would not be poor* (Pearce and McAdoo 1977).

SEX-SEGREGATED EMPLOYMENT

One of the principal causes and facilitators of sex-based wage discrimination is rigid occupational segregation of the workplace into "women's" jobs and "men's" jobs. Twenty years after passage of the Civil Rights Act, the extent of "sex segregation" of the workforce remains staggering. Of the 427 occupational classifications recognized by the U.S. Department of Labor, half of all working women are employed in only twenty (National Committee on Pay Equity undated). In 1982 more than half of all women in the paid workforce were employed in occupations that are 75 percent female, while nearly a quarter of employed women were in jobs that are more than 95 percent female (Bureau of Labor Statistics 1983: table 22).[6] This segregation has a telling effect on women's wages: In 1981 the median earning of women was $12,001, compared to the $20,260 median earning of men (U.S. Department of Labor, Women's Bureau 1982).

As recently confirmed by the prestigious National Academy of Sciences, this high concentration of women in a few low-paying occupations is not the result merely of coincidence or personal choice (Noble 1985: A20). Rather, employer-caused job segregation and sex-based wage discrimination has a long history in the United States (Wertheimer 1977). It began with the virtual exclusion of women from the paid workforce and was followed by women's limited access to a few jobs and lower wages for work they performed, even where both men and women were performing the same jobs. According to Wertheimer (1977: 246),

> When Brooklyn became part of New York City in 1898, the New York legislature set $600 a year as the scale for women teachers . . . and $900 for men. . . . The Interborough Association of Women Teachers . . . [which] organized . . . around the issue of equal pay . . . succeeded in getting an equal pay bill through the legislature, but New York City's mayor disapproved and the law could not take effect. The legislature repassed the bill and this time Governor Charles Evans Hughes vetoed it, pointing out that women were paid less throughout state institutions and that he saw no reason for women who taught in New York City to be treated any differently.

Upton Sinclair wrote eloquently and poignantly of the peculiar plight of working women and their wages. In *The Jungle* (1905: 100–08), he described Marija, a young female who for union activity had been fired from a job in a meat-packing plant. While looking for a new job she heard of an opening for a "beef trimmer." She got the job because the boss saw that she had the muscles of a man, and so he discharged a man and put Marija to do his work, paying her little more than half what he had paid her predecessor (Wertheimer 1977: 224).

These examples, though perhaps extreme, are not mere vestiges of a bygone era. Rather, such arbitrary and discriminatory sex stereotyping of the workforce continues today. For example, in the 1981 case of *Taylor v. Charley Bros.,*[7] a federal court found that a major grocery wholesaler in Pennsylvania engaged in a host of sexually discriminatory employment practices, including intentionally paying female employees substantially less than men in another department simply because the women worked in an all-female department. Similarly, in *Melani v. Board of Higher Education,*[8] the court found that the university had underpaid women at every level.

Historical and persisting wage discrimination also affects substantial numbers of minority workers, particularly women of color. Minority women have traditionally worked in the same occupational groups as white women and therefore suffer from both race and sex discrimination. However, minority women are even more isolated in the workforce than white women. For example, 60 percent of black women work in only two major occupational groups, clerical and

service, and are assigned to the lowest-paid jobs within those occupational categories. This extreme segregation is reflected in earnings:
In 1981 black women were paid 56 cents for every dollar earned by
white men, white women were paid 61 cents, and Hispanic women
were paid only 52 cents (National Committee on Pay Equity and
National Institute for Women of Color, *Women of Color and Pay
Equity*: 1-2).

In the industrial setting, minority women are discriminatorily
concentrated in certain industries and within those industries are
locked into a limited number of occupations. The jobs to which
minority women are assigned are frequently the most physically
demanding, unpleasant, and, as data from those industries reveals,
often extremely dangerous as well.[9] Despite the unpleasant working conditions and the danger to which these workers are subjected,
the same predictable consequence of segregation—disciminatory low
wages—arises for minority jobs, too (see generally Urban Environment Conference 1984).

SEX-BASED WAGE DISCRIMINATION IS ILLEGAL

Clearly, both law and equity demand an end to these illegal practices.
Wage discrimination based on race or sex violates Title VII of the
Civil Rights Act of 1964.[10] This is simply a straightforward affirma-
tion of what Title VII requires: that no one be paid less for the work
that he or she does simply because of race, religion, color, national
origin, or sex. The only issue appropriate for consideration in a wage
discrimination case is whether, because of sex or race, a particular
employer pays occupants of its traditionally female or minority jobs
less than he or she pays or would pay occupants of traditional male
or nonminority jobs. Where this happens, Title VII is violated.

Although the Title VII case law in the area of sex-based wage discrimination is still in its developmental stages, numerous courts have
held that proven acts of intentional discrimination in compensation
violate Title VII. In *County of Washington v. Gunther*,[11] the first
case in which the Supreme Court dealt with the question of prohibited wage discrimination under Title VII, the female plaintiffs (jail
matrons) alleged that the county had undertaken its own objective

evaluation of the worth of their jobs compared to the male position of "guard" and determined that they should be compensated at a rate of 95 percent of the male rate. Notwithstanding that determination, the county set the female wage rate at only 70 percent of the male rate. The plaintiffs alleged that this depression of the wage rate for matrons' jobs was the result of intentional sex-based wage discrimination. While not ruling on these claims because of the posture in which *Gunther* reached it, the U.S. Supreme Court nonetheless made clear that plaintiffs alleging intentional sex-based wage discrimination should have their day in court to prove those claims.

Similarly, in *IUE v. Westinghouse*,[12] (also pending before the Supreme Court with *Gunther*), the company in the late 1930s had established a job evaluation system for the purpose of standardizing wage rates throughout the industry. Male jobs with the same job evaluation scores as female jobs were assigned to parallel labor grades, numbered 1 through 5. However, the pay for the female job with the highest job evaluation score was less than the pay of the male job (common laborer) with the lowest job evaluation score. After Title VII became effective, the explicitly separate male and female scales were abolished, and the classification lines merged. However, the women's jobs were placed at the bottom of the unified classification line, in labor grades 1 through 5. All of the male jobs were classified in labor grades 6 or above. As a result, the wage differential first established in 1940 was perpetuated, and all men, regardless of the positions they occupied, were paid more than all women (that is, the wage rate for the male job with the lowest point value remained greater than the wage rate for the female job with the highest point value).

Gunther and *Westinghouse* present somewhat different factual settings. In *Gunther*, the jobs involved shared a common core of responsibilities, though not enough to render them substantially equal under the Equal Pay Act.[13] By contrast, the women's and men's jobs in *Westinghouse* were entirely different. Yet in neither case was the degree of similarity of the men's and women's jobs considered relevant. Rather, what was relevant to the courts was the plaintiffs' allegations that the employer's payment of lower wages to women's jobs than to men's jobs determined to require a similar composite of skill, effort, responsibility, and working conditions resulted from an intention to discriminate on the basis of sex. It was this apparent sex-based deviation from the results of job evaluation and market surveys to which the courts attached evidentiary significance in *Gunther* and *IUE v. Westinghouse*. The courts indicated that this deviation, falling along pronounced sex lines, might well be the magical element from which an inference of discriminatory intent could be inferred.[14]

The principle argument raised in support of perpetuating wage discrimination is that the "free market" sets wage rates and that the "costs" of correcting discrimination are too substantial for society to bear. However, more than ten years ago the Supreme Court, in *Corning Glass Works v. Brennan*,[15] flatly rejected the "market" as a defense to Equal Pay Act violations. The Court recognized that the pay differential

> reflected a job market in which Corning could pay women less than men for the same work. That the company took advantage of such a situation may be understandable as a matter of economics, but its differential nevertheless became illegal once Congress enacted the principle of equal pay for equal work.[16]

While *Corning Glass* was decided on the basis of the Equal Pay Act, its holding should also encompass Title VII cases. If the "market" is not a defense to an Equal Pay Act violation, there is simply no basis, in law, equity, or logic, to import it into Title VII as a defense to equally egregious and illegal practices.

NOTES

1. Women accounted for more than three-fifths of the increase in the civilian labor force over the past ten years (U.S. Department of Labor 1984: 1).
2. "[F]ifty-six percent of all children under age 18 (32.7 million) had working mothers in the labor force; 48 percent of all children under age six (9.3 million) had working mothers" (U.S. Department of Labor 1984: 3).
3. Women represented 61 percent of all persons over age 16 whose income was below the poverty level in 1983 (U.S. Department of Labor 1984: 2).
4. The solution of a job does appear to work to alleviate poverty among men. Poverty exists in less than 5 percent of all families with children that are headed by a male wage earner (Pearce and McAdoo 1981: 17).
5. Contrary to the assertions of some, the reason for these wage differentials is not that women work fewer years than men. Analysts have suggested

that only 4 percent of the wage gap is the result of shorter job tenure for women (see U.S. Department of Commerce 1984: 24).

6. According to the U.S. Department of Labor in 1983 women accounted for nearly 44 percent of all persons in the civilian labor force. Forty-nine percent of the black workers, 43 percent of all white workers, and 40 percent of all hispanic workers were women (U.S. Department of Labor 1984: 1).

7. 25 F.E.P. Cases 602, 609 (W.D. Pa. 1981).

8. 31 F.E.P. Cases 648 (S.D.N.Y. 1983).

9. "Black workers face 37% more risk of illness and 20% more risk of death due to their jobs than white workers" (Urban Environment Conference 1984).

10. Section 703(a) provides that "it shall be unlawful employment practice for an employer . . . to . . . discriminate against any individual with respect to his compensation, terms, conditions or privileges of employment, because of . . . race, color, religion, sex or national origin."

11. 101 S.C. 2242 (1981).

12. 631 F.2d 1094 (3d Cir. 1980), cert. denied, 452 U.S. 967 (1981).

13. The Equal Pay Act (EPA), 29 U.S.C. section 206(d), bars employers from ·discriminating in pay rates between men and women performing essentially the same jobs within the same establishment. Differentials based on seniority, merit systems, quantity and quality of production, or other non-sex-based factors do not violate the EPA. Because its coverage is limited to "equal work" (that is, jobs that are "substantially equal"), remedying EPA violations addresses only a very limited number and range of instances involving unlawful sex-based wage discrimination.

14. Cases since *Gunther* have received a somewhat mixed reception by the courts. Yet, every single court addressing the issue of whether sex-based wage discrimination cases may go forward in the absence of an "equal work" showing has unequivocally directed that plaintiffs be allowed to prove their claims.

15. 417 U.S. 188 (1974).

16. 417 U.S. at 205.

REFERENCES

National Committee on Pay Equity. Undated. *The Wage Gap: Myths and Facts.* National Committee on Pay Equity: Washington, D.C.

National Committee on Pay Equity and National Institute for Women of Color. Undated. *Women of Color and Pay Equity.* Washington, D.C.: National Committee on Pay Equity.

Noble, Kenneth. 1985. "Low-Paying Jobs Foreseen for Most Working Women." *New York Times* (December 12): A20.

Pearce, D., and H. McAdoo. 1981. *Women and Children: Alone and in Poverty.* Washington, D.C.: Center for National Policy Review.

Urban Environment Conference. 1984. *Reagan, Toxics and Minorities: A Policy Report.* Washington, D.C.: Urban Environment Conference.

U.S. Department of Commerce, Bureau of the Census. 1984. *American Women: Three Decades of Change.* Washington, D.C.: U.S. Government Printing Office.

U.S. Department of Labor, Bureau of Labor Statistics. 1983. *Employment and Earnings.* Washington, D.C.: U.S. Government Printing Office.

U.S. Department of Labor, Women's Bureau. 1982. *Equal Employment Opportunity for Women: U.S. Policies.* Washington, D.C.: U.S. Government Printing Office.

_____. 1984. *20 Facts on Women Workers.* Washington, D.C.: U.S. Government Printing Office.

Wertheimer, B.M. 1977. *We Were There: The Story of Working Women in America.* New York: Pantheon Books.

16 CORPORATE CONCERN FOR WORKING PARENTS

Judy Farrell

On May 25, 1986, dozens of companies across the nation, along with individual citizens, joined together to raise funds to combat hunger in an event known as "Hands Across America." Some companies contributed millions of dollars to participate in this massive demonstration of compassion and concern. Participation on this occasion and in other historically significant events, including the one hundredth anniversary of the Statue of Liberty, clearly illustrates that corporate America's involvement in major social events and in social change has become more evident and increasingly important. Corporate leaders such as Lee Iacocca now are often seen by the public not only as company heads but also as national figures and concerned citizens.

These concerned citizens and their companies need to respond to a major social development that has dramatically affected the lifestyles of many Americans—the transformation of the family unit and the changing composition of the labor force. With the exception of a handful of corporations, U.S. companies have not responded to the changes that have occurred in our most important institution—the family. According to Dr. Sheila B. Kamerman (1983: 1) (professor of social policy at Columbia University),

> The never-implemented recommendations of the White House Conference on Families in 1980 announced as a first priority that employers should become more responsive to the needs of their employees with family responsibilities.

169

. . . Despite growing discussion in the media and a miscellany of conferences, seminars, and workshops, little change of the sort discussed has occurred at the workplace thus far.

Since requests for support of social causes such as the efforts to wipe out hunger, or to repair a national monument, are not controversial corporations acquiesce to them more readily. Nevertheless, the family in the United States today is in need of significant repair and support, and corporate America does have a role to play in this arena. Addressing the issues surrounding work and family conflicts will require not just corporate financial contributions but more basic changes in internal policies such as work schedules and benefits. While companies tend to be benevolent, attentive, and paternalistic regarding family crises, they often bury their heads in the sand when it comes to the daily strains of managing family life.

These strains, however, have become increasingly difficult for their employees to cope with. Although companies might choose to involve themselves in the dilemma that now confronts the U.S. family out of a sense of social responsibility and humanitarianism, it is crucial that corporate America get involved for a more basic reason— self-interest. Providing more supportive services for families would be good for society, good for the economy, good for the United States, and finally, *good for the bottom line.* As William Woodside ("Channeling Energy—and Cash—Into the Community" 1985: F5) (chairman of the American Can Company) put it,

I firmly believe that a corporation exists to profit its shareholders. But if I spread that horizon a little and say the responsibility is to keep the corporation healthy and growing, then I am face to face with social issues that—if not resolved—will make it increasingly difficult for that corporation to thrive in the future.

HOW CAN CORPORATE AMERICA GET INVOLVED?

There are several steps that corporations can take to relieve the tremendous pressures now exerted on employees who must balance both work and family responsibilities. First, corporations must recognize that a growing number of American workers are working parents. Corporate attitudes and policies should reflect an awareness of this new reality. It is now well known that less than 10 percent of U.S. families fit the "traditional" mold of a male breadwinner with a homemaker wife. Most workers no longer have "someone" at home to attend to all the family responsibilities. Many workers are now shouldering a double burden previously unknown in U.S. postindustrial society. Corporate recognition of this fact can facilitate a flow of corporate policies and programs that are of mutual benefit to both the employer and employee.

The second step—once it is acknowledged that the structure of the new U.S. family redefines the daily responsibilities of the U.S. worker—is for companies to develop flexibility in the workplace. This would translate into flexible attitudes, flexible employee benefits packages, and flexibility in the scheduling of work hours, allocation of leave time, and use of vacation time and personal days.

Most company-provided benefits packages were designed with the "traditional" male breadwinner in mind. Such benefits no longer meet the diversified needs of the contemporary U.S. workforce, and in many cases are no longer cost-effective. By providing employees with flexible benefits that include a wide variety of options to choose from, companies can meet the needs of workers while maximizing cost-effectiveness. In the words of Robert F. Wright (Economic Policy Council 1985: 115) (partner at Arthur Andersen & Company): "Flexible benefits are a politically and economically acceptable type of option for employers to consider. I think such plans provide significant potential for addressing the changing needs of workers."

Companies can also be more flexible in the scheduling of work hours through such programs as flextime, job-sharing, and part-time employment (see Nollen 1982). Since most children have both parents in the workforce today, there is no longer one parent at home to shuttle the kids off to school or to attend to a sick child. By relaxing the traditional rigidity inherent in work schedules, companies can reduce stress, improve morale, and increase productivity through lower rates of absenteeism and turnover. Additionally, because most parent workers cannot predict some of the "family crises" that do occur, it would be important to offer workers flexibility in their use of personal and vacation time.

Another step that corporate America can take to protect the institution of the family is to participate actively in the campaign for affordable, high-quality child care. The children of today are the workers of tomorrow, and companies can invest in human resources by ensuring the quality of care that children receive. At the same time they would be helping to relieve the anxieties that many workers face in the struggle to piece together child care arrangements.

There are many ways for companies to support the development and delivery of child care services (see Chapter 8). Besides providing direct and indirect assistance, companies could involve themselves in efforts to obtain adequate funding from federal, state, and local governments; to coordinate and deliver services; and to enforce standards. American corporations already employ lobbyists to work in the nation's Capitol on behalf of their corporate interests. Shouldn't these same corporations make employees and their families one of their primary interests? As Dana Friedman (Economic Policy Council 1985: 86) (senior research associate at the Conference Board) remarked:

> There are other ways for corporate America to get involved. For instance, government relations departments of corporations could pay attention to the public system of child care. If companies had been aware of the impact that recent federal cutbacks have had on their own employees, then they might have joined forces with others who were working to prevent those kinds of cutbacks and the resulting problems. In addition, if the basic service structure were in place, it would be easier for corporations to expand and improve it.

The steps outlined above offer starting points for companies to consider as they reshape corporate policies that take into account the current composition of the labor force and the dramatic transformation of the family. A few exceptional companies have adopted human resource policies and implemented benefits programs that demonstrate an awareness of and sensitivity to the demands placed on the working parent. Many of these policies were developed in workplaces where innovative corporate leaders responded with vision and purpose to the socioeconomic changes that have swept the United States in recent years—changes that have profoundly affected the lifestyles of workers and their families. Unfortunately, the reports of exciting new company-sponsored programs that assist working parents seem to include the same names over and over again. The following summary of successful corporate efforts to address the needs of working parents might provide a generic model for other companies to follow.

Merck & Co.

Merck, headquartered in Rahway, New Jersey, is the largest ethical pharmaceutical company in the United States (Economic Policy Council 1985: 125–35). The company has twenty-six plants in the United States, fifty-one plants overseas, and twelve experimental farms and research laboratories in eighteen locations around the world. Merck employs 35,000 people—16,500 of whom are based in the United States. Merck has implemented a number of policies and practices that are responsive to family-life demands and changed life-styles.

For over thirty years, Merck has had a maternity leave policy that currently provides a leave of absence from work for up to eighteen months. The mother is paid during the period of disability (about six weeks). After an absence of six months, the employee will be returned to the previous position wherever feasible or to one of like status and pay. For absences of more than six months and less than eighteen months, the company will provide a return to employment, but the employee may not be granted the former position or one of like status. However, every effort will be made to place the employee in a position that is consistent with the employee's qualifications. Leaves after the period of disability are without pay, but with medical and dental coverage for up to eighteen months.

In late 1978 Merck began discussions with a group of employees at its Rahway headquarters who had indicated an interest in more readily available day care. A feasibility study was conducted, and in 1980 the Employee's Center for Young Children was opened near the Rahway work site. Merck was instrumental in providing start-up funding, advice, and guidance during the organization phase of this center, and Merck continues to provide a variety of "in kind" services (such as telephone and printing of brochures) and advice.

At the company's second-largest location in West Point, Pennsylvania, Merck used another approach. A number of already existing child care centers were in place in relative proximity to the West Point facility. However, their space was limited and therefore provided little availability to Merck employees. After extensive research into the quality of care provided by these centers and the credentials of the operators, Merck selected one to be the recipient of a company grant in exchange for preferential admission for Merck employees. The Merck grant also enabled the center to expand its services and facilities.

In an effort to provide additional flexibility to employees for whom family demands were more frequently clashing with work demands, Merck instituted flextime at many of its locations. Flextime, not specifically designed as a family support approach, allows all employees to handle more effectively personal demands (as well as recreational or scholastic activities) during the normal workday hours, while at the same time preserving the total hours worked by the employee. Merck has found that flextime not only offers benefits to the employee but shows evidence of benefits to the company in the form of reduced need for personal time off. Employees at Merck work a "regular" day in terms of hours worked, but they may begin work as early as 7:00 A.M. or as late as 9:30 A.M.

Merck has tested a number of other alternate work arrangements and two approaches that are being used with increased frequency are flexplace and part-time work. Flexplace allows the employee on maternity leave to begin the transition back to work earlier and at the same time allows the employee an opportunity to handle demands that continue in the home setting.

Merck recognizes that a wide range of medical, behavioral, personal, and family difficulties and needs can potentially affect an employee's productivity on the job. Merck believes that although the company cannot answer all of the needs of the employee, it should provide appropriate flexibility, support, and in the case of major problems an extra measure of understanding. The company can also direct the employee to appropriate outside agencies that have the expertise necessary to address a particular personal problem. The Merck Employee Assistance Program provides confidential counseling for a wide range of problems—alcoholism and drug abuse, family and marital difficulties, legal and financial worries.

Merck's approach to family support policies and practices recognizes that the life of the average employee has become increasingly more complex over recent years. As Arthur Strohmer, Merck's director of Human Resources Staffing and Development, pointed out,

As people's lives have changed, so must the corporation's adaptation to these changed life patterns evolve to a point where there is a useful integration between an employee's family life and work life. This integration is an important factor in the employee's maintaining a life that is fulfilling and in the corporation's maintaining a productive and focused work force.

American Can Company

The American Can Company realized in the late 1970s that its traditional benefits program no longer met the needs of the contemporary U.S. family (Economic Policy Council 1985: 136–38). The company was also concerned about the escalating costs of benefits and set out to redesign its benefits program. A flexible benefits plan appeared to be the ideal way for American Can to meet the dual objectives of satisfying employees' needs and allowing the company to manage the increasing costs of benefits.

A flexible benefits plan establishes a core package of benefits that provide a basic level of security and a level of flexible credits that allow employees to purchase additional benefits that meet their individual needs. These options range from savings benefits and health, life, and disability insurance to vacation, day care, and financial planning. Based on its experience thus far, American Can believes that:

1. An existing benefits program can be split into nonflexible and flexible portions in a cost-effective way rather than merely adding flexibility on top of an existing high-cost benefits package;

2. Deductibles for medical benefits are acceptable. Ninety percent of American Can's workers found deductibles acceptable if the dollars saved could be spent in another form; and

3. A large organization can establish and administer a flexible benefits program with a wide variety of choices.

The response to American Can's flexible benefits program has been extremely positive, and a 1982 survey of employees found that 72 percent rated the program as either very good or excellent. American Can attributes much of this program's success to the opportunity it affords employees to make their own choices, to the role it gives them in the decisionmaking process, and to its potential for helping the employer to control future increases in benefits costs.

Steelcase, Inc.

Steelcase, the world's leading designer and manufacturer of office systems furniture and office lighting, employs 8,000 people at its corporate headquarters in Grand Rapids, Michigan (Economic Policy Council 1985: 139–48). Steelcase's commitment to its employees and their families is inherent in the company's philosophy that the key to corporate success is threefold: (1) identifying the needs of people; (2) balancing individual group needs for the mutual satisfaction of all groups; and (3) supporting the individual group needs for the collective benefit of all the groups. Steelcase is a family-owned company employing over 400 working couples and four generations of families.

Good labor relations, enhanced through a family-oriented benefits program, are the reasons why Steelcase has never had a labor-initiated work stoppage since the company was founded in 1912. In fact, Steelcase's turnover rate is less than 4 percent, one-half the national average.

Steelcase's many employee benefits and policies include an in-house counseling service, preretirement counseling, flexible benefits with a child care reimbursement account, a rehabilitation program, a recreation program, a wellness program, nutrition-oriented food services, career counseling, a van-pool program, flex- and part-time work schedules, summer employment for employee's children, job security, and profit sharing. In addition, Steelcase initiated a comprehensive child care service in 1980.

The Child Care Service is a branch of the Human Resources' Employee Information and Services Department. It is staffed by two full-time child care coordinators. The goal of the service is to assist Steelcase employees in maintaining and/or improving the quality of their family lives. The Child Care Service accomplishes this goal by providing services that help employees, as parents and parents-to-be, to obtain a balance between work and family responsibilities. The Child Care Service provides childrearing information, referral to care-givers, parent education seminars, technical assistance to child care programs, and advocacy for families and children. The referral component of the Child Care Service matches employee child care needs to community child care programs and works with those programs to increase the quality and variety of child care available. Since its inception, the Child Care Service has experienced a steady increase in use by employees. A survey of those employees using the service found that most felt it had a positive effect on their ability to perform, and 94 percent felt more productive at work.

Steelcase also has an ongoing relationship with and offers many kinds of assistance to child care providers who serve Steelcase families. A monthly newsletter offers new insights and practical tips on child care. Participation in the Steelcase Child Case Service network helps providers develop professionally and overcome the isolation that some feel. The Child Care Service also lends providers essential equipment such as cribs, high chairs, infant car seats, and educational materials.

The child care coordinators are also active in community organizations that serve families and children. They work closely with agencies such as the Department of Social Services Division of Child Day Care Licensing, Community Coordinated Child Care, Family Day Care Association, Association for the Education of Young Children, and the Center Directors' Association, and they confer with other employers involved in supporting child care. Steelcase sponsored a conference for other employers to share the success of their Child Care Initiative in 1984.

HOW WILL CORPORATE AMERICA BENEFIT FROM GETTING INVOLVED?

Many experts believe that employer responsiveness to family needs does increase productivity, although there is no hard evidence to support this theory. Evidence does exist that benefits such as flextime and flexible benefits plans improve employee morale and help in recruitment and retention of employees (Kamerman 1983: 17).

As we have seen from the preceding case studies, Merck's experience demonstrates that family support policies and practices significantly reduce employee stress and this positively affects the employee's productivity on the job. Furthermore, American Can's approach is evidence that flexible benefits plans have the potential to eliminate waste, while at the same time meeting employees' needs. Finally, policies and benefits at Steelcase illustrate how family support services can be good investments that yield loyalty, commitment, and pride in job performance.

178 FAMILY AND WORK

CONCLUSION

The needs of workers and their families can become a national priority if the corporate community commits itself to that goal. Companies can create human resource policies that are responsive to these needs and also can become an effective voice in advocating national policies that support and strengthen the family. Thanks to the vision and boldness of a few corporate citizens, companies have some exemplary models to build on.

By reaching out to workers and their families—and by working with other actors in the community such as unions, the schools, child care programs, and local, state, and federal governments—corporate America can help bridge some of the gaps between work and family life. In so doing, the corporate community would be helping to strengthen the foundation of the family unit, a vital component of national stability and international competitiveness.

REFERENCES

Economic Policy Council. 1985. *Work and Family in the United States: A Policy Initiative.* New York: UNA-USA.

Kamerman, Sheila B. 1983. *Meeting Family Needs: The Corporate Response.* New York: Pergamon Press, Work in America Institute Studies in Productivity.

"Channeling Energy—and Cash—Into the Community." 1985. *New York Times* (September 29): F5.

Nollen, Stanley D. 1982. *New Work Schedules in Practice: Managing Time in a Changing Society.* New York: Van Nostrand Reinhold/Work in America Institute Series.

17 THE U.S. LABOR MOVEMENT AND WORKING WOMEN
An Alliance for the Future

Pamela Laber

The U.S. labor movement is at a critical juncture. In the words of Lane Kirkland, president of the AFL–CIO, "What we in the American labor force face is not a passing period of acute crisis. Rather we face a permanent challenge to our basic role in American life" ("Union on the Run" 1981: 61).

Over the past decade organized labor has suffered massive membership losses in its traditional power base, the industrial unions. Fierce foreign competition has spurred many industries to shift production to low-wage countries and to introduce labor-saving technology. Coupled with several severe recessions, the result has been exceptionally high levels of unemployment, especially in manufacturing industries. The AFL–CIO lost 2.7 million members between 1980 and 1984. Union membership has declined steadily since its peak of 35 percent of the labor force in 1944, and the decline has accelerated since 1970 when unions represented 27.3 percent of the labor force; in 1985 fewer than 19 percent of U.S. workers belonged to a union ("Why Unions Are Running Scared" 1984: 62).

Declining union membership has not been uniform across all sectors of the economy. Unions in heavy industries have suffered the largest losses. The United Automobile Workers of America membership has dropped 27 percent (a total of 450,000 workers) since the 1970s, and the Steelworkers have seen a 45 percent decline in their membership since 1980 ("Union Membership Falls Sharply" 1983: 42). Murray Seeger, director of public information for the AFL–CIO,

179

reports that of the ninety-six unions affiliated with the AFL-CIO, thirty-seven are declining and thirty are growing. The growth unions like the American Federation of State, County, and Municipal Employees (AFSCME), the Service Employees International Union (SEIU), the Office and Professional Employees International Union, and the United Food and Commercial Workers Union (Seeger 1984) are primarily in the public sector and service industries where employment is growing rapidly.

In the recession-riddled, deregulated world of the late 1970s and early 1980s, unions (from auto and steel to airlines and public employees) granted unprecedented wage and benefit concessions at the bargaining table. These concessions were hailed as beginning a new era of cooperation between labor and management, but some observers view these "give backs" as a fundamental shift in power to employers from unions. Just how far the balance was tipped is now being revealed. Labor is winning only a limited share of the gains to be reaped from the economic recovery, relative to the extent that they shared in the losses of the 1981-82 recession.

In addition to the structural and cyclical economic trends that have worked to erode organized labor's power base, labor is currently operating in an openly hostile political environment. The Reagan administration initially made clear its stand on organized labor by dismissing 12,000 striking air traffic controllers and decertifying their union in August 1981. In addition, Reagan political appointees named to top positions on the National Labor Relations Board have been openly antagonistic toward the labor movement. Some analysts claim that the image of the AFL-CIO has been so maligned that their endorsement of Walter Mondale's 1984 candidacy for president not only did not help him to win but even may have cost him the election.

The political influence of organized labor is at low ebb and apparently so too their appeal to the average worker in the United States. Unions currently win less than 43 percent of representation elections, compared with winning 55 percent of these elections in 1970 and 94 percent in 1937 ("Why Unions Are Running Scared" 1984: 64). Union decertification drives are successful 75 percent of the time, and in 1982, 682 union locals were decertified ("Unionists See Labor Day '84 1984"). These trends are partially the result of stepped up antiunion activity on the part of employers. But the contract concessions and other strategies adopted by numerous unions con-

fronted with intractably high unemployment in the wake of the recession, have been seen by many rank and file union members as the
leadership "selling out" and helping the company at the expense of
the worker's wages and the union's power. As one UAW member put
it, "the union [leaders] don't work for our interests. They are just
another power structure. Just like Uncle Sam taking our taxes, the
union takes our dues and doesn't do anything for us."

The disaffection among many union members is understandable.
The foundation of organized labor's appeal to workers has always
been higher wages and better benefits. Yet average annual union
wage increases have been declining, and in 1983 union wage rates
increased on the average by only 2.8 percent. This was the lowest
annual percentage increase in the sixteen years for which records
have been kept, and was lower than the average raises awarded to
most nonunion workers in that year ("Why Unions Are Running
Scared" 1984: 63). A 1984 strike by workers at Disneyland was
termed victorious because their new contract included a two-year
wage freeze but no *cut* in benefits ("Disneyland Workers Return as
Strike Ends" 1984). A bitter 1985 strike by TWA flight attendants
was waged over the percentage *reduction* in salary the attendants
were willing to accept. These are just a few vivid examples of the loss
of power and defensive approach that has been adopted by much of
the labor movement.

The perception of the union leadership in the eyes of the rank and
file has been tarnished further by the tactics of many unions. Often
labor leaders seem to show more sensitivity to the economic plight
of the industry they bargain with than of the workers the unions
presumably represent. For example, the Communications Workers
of America (CWA) is spending its own money for television commer-
cials to help market AT&T's long distance service. They hope to save
union jobs by keeping AT&T's new nonunion competitors (MCI,
Sprint, and so forth) from wresting a large market share away from
AT&T. A stronger union approach would have been for the CWA to
organize the workers at AT&T's competitors rather than pay for part
of AT&T's advertising expenses.

Some CWA members are dismayed by the union's current tactics.
One member who has worked for AT&T for eleven years and is a
member of the executive committee of her CWA local conceded that

I feel we [the CWA] have a responsibility to organize the new phone company competitors. The workers at MCI and Sprint, you know, to try to gain

members from within the industry and also to keep our wages higher. There is talk about organizing these people, but so far nothing has been done.

In a past era, it is certain that the CWA would have been organizing the unorganized rather than buying TV time for Ma Bell.

Many union leaders are now claiming that their unions have made a new commitment to organizing. However, organizing in the 1980s is unlike organizing at any previous time, and for many reasons it will be very difficult. To begin with, organized labor in this country is under attack, and not only must it make up for numerical membership losses, but it must combat a bad public image — among its members, potential members, and society in general. A member of the New York State Public Employees Federation maintains that "there's not a tremendous amount of pride among union members about belonging to a union, like there once was. They don't see it as a positive thing." Al Viani from AFSCME's DC 37 concedes that "The population at large has a very negative attitude towards trade unions. We have to change that." Viani believes that "There has to be some solid soul-searching within the movement. There is a great need for some structural and procedural changes within the unions and within the movement." According to John Sweeney of the SEIU, "organizing is ultimately where we [the labor movement] will win or lose" ("Why Unions Are Running Scared" 1984: 62), and Murray Seeger, director of public information at the AFL-CIO, agrees that rebuilding labor's ranks is critical and that "The future of labor is women and minorities."

In the past three decades there has been a large-scale entry of women into the labor force, and the percentage of women who work outside the home has soared from 34 percent in 1950 to 64 percent today. Forty-five percent of the labor force is female, and in 1984 for the first time white men (the traditional source of union members) did not make up the majority of the workplace ("Shifts in Work Put White Men in a Minority" 1984: 1). Since 1970 nearly two-thirds of all new workers have been women, and this will continue to be true through 1995 ("Shifts in Work" 1984: 1). Women have accounted for over half of all union member growth since 1966 ("Getting Organized" 1979) and now comprise 28 percent of all union members (Seeger 1984). Historically the relationship between women and labor unions has been limited at best. But today there is both the need and the possibility for unions and women to develop a new and mutually beneficial relationship.

A recent Harris poll indicates that there is a "special receptivity" to unions among minorities, younger workers, and women—especially those who work for companies with fewer than one hundred employees in fields such as finance, insurance, real estate, and retail trade. Whereas 63 percent of all Americans reportedly would vote no if a union election were held at their workplace tomorrow, 44 percent of all women would vote yes ("Beyond Unions" 1985: 22).

This "receptivity" may be due to the fact that women in the labor force work for precisely the same reason that men do—because they have to. Seventy percent of working women are single, separated, divorced, widowed, or married to men who earn less than $15,000 a year. Yet the average woman worker in the United States has earned less than two-thirds of the male wage, regardless of occupation, since time immemorial, and only one in ten women earns over $20,000 a year (Goldsmith 1984: 34). Women workers, as a group, could benefit greatly from the traditional union promises of higher wages and benefits, recourse against discrimination and unfair management actions, and a modicum of job security. Unions, meanwhile, are looking for new members.

There is tremendous potential for an alliance to develop between women and organized labor. Already hints of this potential have been raised by recent strike actions by predominantly female workers determined to stand up for their rights—such as the strike by clerical workers at Yale University in the fall of 1984. Yet before women will swell the ranks of U.S. labor unions, unions must begin to take up the issues of special concern to women workers in a forceful way.

The issues that are important to working women intersect to a certain degree with the issues that concern all workers, such as good wages and benefits, health and safety, job protection, and pension rights. There are, however, a category of concerns that are of particular interest to women—and increasingly to some men—that have to do with the discrimination women encounter in the labor market and with integrating work and family life in a satisfactory way. These issues include pay equity, maternity and parental leaves and benefits, child care, and flexible working hours. These are issues that most unions to date have been hesitant if not outright unwilling to consider seriously.

In U.S. society there is a prevalent attitude that issues related to the individual in the family are purely personal issues and that issues related to the employee in the workplace are the responsibility of the employer and employee or the employee's bargaining agent. There is little recognition that the activities that take place both at home and in the workplace are social activities and that society therefore has some collective responsibility for them. This social responsibility is recognized throughout the rest of the industrialized world, and women's family responsibilities are understood to be why on the one hand they have to work outside the home and on the other hand they are disadvantaged in the labor market. All industrialized countries, besides the United States, provide health care to pregnant women and infants, have statutory rights to maternity and parenting leaves and benefits, provide economic assistance of different kinds to young families, and have at least acknowledged the need and begun to develop affordable quality child care. These programs not only benefit children, but they go a long way toward reducing the stresses and underlying factors of discrimination women encounter in the labor market.

In the United States 54 percent of married women are employed (U.S. Congress 1984: 1) and in 1984, 61 percent of women with children under age 18 were in the labor force, as were 60 percent with children between ages 3 and 5, 50 percent with children under age 3, and 48 percent with children less than one year old (Kamerman 1984).

With organized labor's traditional constituency shrinking and its role in U.S. life as both legitimate and necessary being questioned, some segments of the labor movement are beginning to contemplate new strategies based on new premises and a new constituency. Women workers provide an ample pool from which to build a new membership base, and issues like child care, maternity leaves, pay equity, and flexible work hours are exciting issues that could prove especially successful in organizing women. The social nature of these issues enables unions to approach them in innovative ways. For example, by involving the community in the provision of child care unions can increase the likelihood of obtaining employer child care assistance at the bargaining table. Such activities will also place the union movement at the forefront of positive social change and help to broaden their base of political support as they become recognized as leaders in the public interest, working to provide needed services to their members and their communities.

The challenge before organized labor is clear, but there is no easy road to take. It is true that a few assertive unions have begun to take on new issues in response to their membership and a changing political and economic environment. For example, AFSCME and the SEIU have led the growing struggle for equal pay and comparable worth, and the New York City Local 23-25 of the International Ladies Garment Workers Union (ILGWU) has opened a child care center in conjunction with the employer group they bargain with, community groups, and the city. Yet overall, union structure and machinery and many union leaders are deeply entrenched and work to preserve the status quo. This is a large part of why organized labor has reacted to change so slowly and defensively. Yet if organized labor in the United States does not want to become just part of our folklore, these obstacles will have to be overcome. If unions begin to act, and act creatively and aggressively, in response to the changes occurring around them, a formidable challenge could be turned into a great opportunity, and a new chapter in U.S. labor history may be written.

REFERENCES

"Beyond Unions: A Revolution in Employee Rights in the Making." 1985. *Business Week* (July 8).

"Disneyland Workers Return as Strike Ends." 1984. *New York Times* (October 18).

"Getting Organized: More Women Enroll in Unions." 1979. *Wall Street Journal* (January 15).

Goldsmith, Judy. 1984. *Testimony before the House Subcommittee on Compensation and Employee Benefits of the Committee on Post Office and Civil Service.* 98th Cong., 2nd Sess. (April 3).

Kamerman, Sheila B. 1984. Remarks at the Economic Policy Council Plenary Session, Washington, D.C., September 14.

Seeger, Murray. 1984. Interview with author.

"Shifts in Work Put White Men in a Minority." 1984. *New York Times* (July 31): 1.

"Unionists See Labor Day '84." 1984. *New York Times* (September 3).

"Union on the Run." 1981. *U.S. Nrws & World Report* (September 14): 61.

U.S. House Select Committee on Children, Youth, and Families. 1984. Hearing on *Families and Child Care: Improving the Options.* 98th Cong. Serial 98-109. September 17.

"Why Unions Are Running Scared." 1984. *U.S. News & World Report* (September 10): 62.

18 CONCLUSIONS
A Policy Agenda for the United States

Sylvia Ann Hewlett

In the spring of 1983 the Economic Policy Council (EPC) of the United Nations Association set up a panel on family policy in America. The mission of the group was to investigate the problems facing working parents and to recommend policy measures that would help resolve them. The central idea was that family life in this country is in the midst of revolutionary change and that this has major economic as well as social implications. The panel was funded by the Ford and Rockefeller foundations, and chaired by John Sweeney (president of SEIU, the Service Employees International Union) and Alice Ilchman (president, Sarah Lawrence College). During its lifespan the panel involved the energies of such eminent individuals as Gerald Ford (former president), Katherine Graham (chairman, the Washington Post Company), Gerald McEntree (president, AFSCME), and Robert O. Anderson (chairman, the Atlantic Richfield Company).

The EPC project was intended to produce realistic solutions, not pie in the sky. The panel members, while sympathetic to the problems at hand, were not professional do-gooders but hard-headed members of the establishment who had a firm grip on economic and political reality. The goal was to find out what could be done for American families in the mid-1980s, an era of budget cutting and limited social conscience.

In January 1986 the EPC released its report at a Senate dinner hosted by Senators Moynihan, Mathias, and Lugar. At this event seventy-five high-ranking corporate and labor union executives signed off on a set of family support policies they deemed feasible. The report, *Work and Family in the United States: A Policy Initiative*, contained the following recommendations:

1. Maternity and Parental Leave. The EPC panel endorsed the following package: (1) Federal legislation mandating temporary disability insurance in the forty-five states that currently do not require such coverage. (2) An expansion of the definition of disability to give women the right to at least six to eight weeks' leave at the time of birth with some wage replacement during this time and a job guarantee at the end of the period. (3) A unpaid, job-protected parenting leave for either parent for up to six months after birth.

2. Maternity and Child Health. The EPC panel recommended that the federal government give priority to health coverage for pregnant women and children. Not only are these two groups disproportionately impoverished and disproportionately uninsured, but there is extensive evidence that increases in preventative maternal and child health care reap substantial long-range savings in catastrophic care programs.

3. Flexible Work Schedules and Career Ladders. The EPC panel emphasized that working parents of small children need time to spend together. Employers should therefore be encouraged to make more work-sharing and part-time employment available at all occupational levels, including management, without curtailing the promotional opportunities of employees. Flextime should be implemented on a larger scale to allow employees to better integrate work and family responsibilities, and special leave time for parents to care for sick children should be established. Traditional career paths should be assessed in relation to the family responsibilities of working parents, since more and more men and women in traditional career trajectories find that the most critical phases of their work and family lives coincide.

4. Preschool and Early Childhood Education. The EPC panel pointed out that in the United States today there are approximately 8.5 million children under age 6 with working parents and that preschool can play a much-needed and valuable role in

boosting the quality of early childhood education and in meeting child care needs. By making preschool available on a voluntary basis to ages 3–5, and by extending the school day, the public school system could serve important educational and child care objectives. In addition, school facilities should be used for be-fore- and after-school programs. Such policies would reduce the need for, and therefore the cost of, remedial education programs.

5. Child Care. In the interest of realism, the recommendations of the Economic Policy Council in the sphere of child care were modest. (1) Public Sector Initiatives. The variety of programs through which the U.S. government currently subsidizes child care is very limited. Still, it seems unlikely at this time, when gov-ernment is reducing spending on all social programs, that there will be any significant increase in direct funding for child care. However, funding for such programs as Title XX of the Social Security Act should be restored and even expanded. In addition, the Child Care Tax Credit should be broadened and made refund-able so that low-income families can also benefit from it. (2) Private Sector Initiatives. A growing number of companies are interested in organizing or subsidizing child care programs, and the private sector could become an important source of child care in this country. Labor unions, community groups, and cor-porations should be encouraged to develop child care services through government tax policy and other official incentives.

The EPC report on family policy captured headlines across the nation. The *New York Times* and the *Washington Post* ran feature articles as did the *Los Angeles Times*, the *Cleveland Plain Dealer*, and South Carolina's *The State*. The report hit a nerve; for the first time an influential group of business and labor leaders were taking these family issues seriously and recommending policy solutions that both made economic sense and were acceptable to the private sector.

The *Washington Post* described the work of the EPC policy panel in the following terms (Mann 1986):

> The report is not a wish list from working mothers. Far from it. It is a hard-nosed analysis of what is needed to improve the productivity and economic well-being of the current work force. . . . The panel put forth the most con-vincing argument of all for its recommendations: In the long- and the short-run they are cost effective.

Family policy is emerging as one of the most critical political issues of the mid-1980s for the simple reason that the majority of Americans are experiencing tremendous strain as their work and family lives increasingly conflict. New tensions have arisen from the massive structural changes that have swept through the mainstream of American society. Today, 45 percent of the labor force is female, and married women with young children comprise the majority of new entrants to the job market. Indeed, 50 percent of babies under 1 year old now have mothers in the workplace.

Yet economic and social policymaking in the United States still assumes that the "traditional family" is the dominant family type. This despite the fact that in 1986 fewer than 10 percent of American families fit the traditional Norman Rockwell mold—breadwinning husband, homemaking wife, and one or more dependent children. Not only do both parents in most married-couple families work, but the number of single-parent households headed by women has increased rapidly with the growing frequency of divorce and unwed motherhood. Most children in the United States today have working mothers, and most parents must balance the competing demands of work and family responsibilities. It is high time that government and business recognize these new realities and respond to them with supportive family policies.

The evidence suggests that the pressures created by shifts in family structure and labor force participation will intensify in the future. Over the last decade, two-thirds of all new entrants into the labor force have been women, and this is likely to remain the case through the 1990s. By the year 2000 half of the workforce will be female and over half of all workers will be parents with children at home. The United States is also headed toward a labor shortage. Recent studies predict that the labor force growth rate may fall to 3 percent between 1990 and 1995 (down from a growth rate of 10 percent between 1975 and 1980). This means that individual companies will be facing increasing competition in attracting and retaining the best workers and increasing pressure to provide such things as quality child care and flexible career ladders. Maintaining traditional policies in the workplace and in government will begin to limit efficiency and economic growth. In short, training programs, benefits systems, career ladders, and work rules all need to be reoriented to respond to what is now the typical American employee: the worker with significant parental responsibilities.

Throughout the developed world changes in workforce and family patterns, similar to those in the United States, have been occurring. Most countries have responded by implementing a coordinated set of public and private policies that bolster parents and their children. Among industrialized countries, the United States is conspicuous for its failure to respond to this massive structural shift. It is time our policies caught up with these in the rest of the world. The competitive strength of our economy and the health and well-being of American family life are at stake.

REFERENCE

1. Mann, Judy. 1986. "Women and the Work Force." *The Washington Post.* January 22.

INDEX

PROJECT PANEL
AND PARTICIPANTS

207

Members: (*continued*)

GERALD R. FORD
Former President
United States of America

DANA E. FRIEDMAN
Senior Research Fellow
The Conference Board

ELI GINZBERG
Director, Conservation
of Human Resources
Columbia University

RUTH J. HINERFELD
Past President
League of Women Voters of
the United States

LAWRENCE HUGHES
President
The Hearst Trade Book Group

FREDRICK W. HUSZAGH
Professor of Law
University of Georgia
Law School

SHEILA B. KAMERMAN
Professor of Social Policy
Columbia University School
of Social Work

MARK J. MAGED
Partner
Holtzmann, Wise & Shepard

RAY MARSHALL
Bernard Rapoport Professor of
Economics and Public Affairs
University of Texas at Austin

GERALD W. McENTEE
International President
American Federation of State,
County and Municipal
Employees, AFL-CIO

JOYCE MILLER
Vice President
Amalgamated Clothing and Textile
Workers Union, AFL-CIO

HENRY NICHOLAS
President
National Union of Hospital and
Health Care Employees,
RWDSU/AFL-CIO

REX R. REED
Former Senior Vice President,
Labor Relations and Corporate
Personnel
AT&T

STEVEN J. ROSS
Chairman and Chief Executive Officer
Warner Communications, Inc.

ROBERT D. SCHMIDT
Chairman
Earth Energy Systems, Inc.

PATRICK J. SCOLLARD
Executive Vice President,
Human Resources
Chemical Bank

ALBERT SHANKER
President
American Federation of Teachers,
AFL-CIO

WALTER TROSIN
Vice President for Human Resources
Merck & Co., Inc.

ROSALIE J. WOLF
Treasurer
International Paper Company

Additional Participants:

OLGA BAUDELOT
Institut National de Recherche
  et de Documentation
Pedagogique, Paris

PHOEBE COTTINGHAM
Assistant Director
Social Sciences Division
Rockefeller Foundation

MARIAN WRIGHT EDELMAN
President
Children's Defense Fund

ELLEN GALLINSKY
Project Director
Work and Family Life Study
Bank Street College

KATHARINE GRAHAM
Chairman of the Board
The Washington Post Company

ROBERT GRANGER
Vice President and Dean
School and Community Services
Bank Street College

JOY ANN GRUNE
Former Executive Director
National Committee on Pay Equity

ELINOR GUGGENHEIMER
President
Child Care Action Campaign

MOLLY HARDY
Executive Director, Empire
State Day Care Services Corp.

HEIDI I. HARTMANN
Study Director
National Academy of Science's
  Committee on Women's Employ-
  ment and Related Social Issues

ALEXIS HERMAN
Vice President
Green-Herman and Associates, Inc.

BETTY HOLMES
Representative
United Federation of Teachers,
  AFL-CIO

SOL HURWITZ
Senior Vice President
Committee for Economic
  Development

CAL JETER
Director of Employee Services
  and Information
Steelcase, Inc.

JEROME KAGAN
Professor of Psychology
Harvard University

CAROL KIRSCH
Employee Relations Coordinator
Time, Inc.

ANNA-GRETA LEIJON
Minister of Labor
Sweden

LEE LEVIN
Executive Director
Coalition of Labor Union Women
  (CLUW)

PAUL MOYER
Manager of Executive Compensation
General Electric Company

WINN NEWMAN
Newman, Sobol, Trister & Owens

MARY ROSE OAKAR
Member
United States Congress

BARNEY OLMSTED
Co-Director
New Ways to Work

FRANCES FOX PIVEN
Professor of Political Science
CUNY Graduate Center

Additional Participants: (*continued*)

DIANA ROCK
Director of Women's Rights and
  Community Action Programs
AFSCME

ISABEL SAWHILL
Senior Fellow
The Urban Institute

GERRY SHEA
Director, Healthcare Division
Service Employees International
  Union, AFL-CIO-CLC

PETER J. SLOANE
Head of Department
Political Economy
University of Aberdeen, Scotland

ARTHUR F. STROHMER, JR.
Executive Director, Human
  Resources Staffing and
  Development
Merck & Co., Inc.

AMY VANCE
Program Officer
Ford Foundation

PAT WARD
Child Care Coordinator
Steelcase, Inc.

EPC Staff

DANIEL F. BURTON, JR.
Executive Director

ROSE CARCATERRA
Program Director

MARIA D. RIVERA
Secretary

ABOUT THE CONTRIBUTORS

Olga Baudelot is a researcher at the National Institute of Pedagogical Research (INRP) of the Ministry of Education in Paris and a member of the CRESAS Research Team (Centre de Recherche d'Education spécialisée et d'Adaptation scolaire), working on early childhood educational issues.

Mario Matthew Cuomo is the Governor of New York and Chairman of the National Governor's Association Task Force on the Homeless. He began public service in January 1975 when Governor Hugh L. Carey appointed him Secretary of State. In 1978 Cuomo was elected Lieutenant Governor and added the responsibilities of Chairman of the State's Urban and Rural Affairs Cabinets as well as the State Advisory Council on the Disabled.

Cuomo was graduated summa cum laude from St. John's University in 1953 and tied for top of the class honors at St. John's University School of Law in 1956. In 1956 he became confidential legal assistant to Judge Adrian P. Burke of the New York State Court of Appeals, and entered private practice of law in 1958 with the firm of Corner, Weisbrod, Froeb and Charles. Mr. Cuomo simultaneously taught at St. John's Law School as an adjunct professor for seventeen years and served as chairman of the St. John's University Alumni Federation. His published works include *Diaries of Mario M. Cuomo: The Campaign for Governor* (1984) and *Forest Hills Diary: The Crisis of Low-Income Housing* (1974).

Marian Wright Edelman is founder and President of the Children's Defense Fund in Washington, D.C. A graduate of Spelman College and Yale Law School, Ms. Edelman started and directed the NAACP Legal Defense and Education Fund Office in Jackson, Mississippi, and was the first black woman admitted to the Mississippi bar. In 1968 she founded the Washington Research Project, a public interest law firm and the parent body of the Children's Defense Fund. Mrs. Edelman was named by *Time* magazine in 1971 as one of America's 200 young leaders and by the *Ladies Home Journal* in 1983 as one of the 100 most influential women in America. In 1985 she was named a MacArthur Foundation Prize Fellow. Ms. Edelman holds honorary degrees from twenty-five universities and colleges.

Judy Farrell is Project Coordinator of the Economic Policy Council. Prior to joining the EPC staff in 1981, she was assistant to the Alateen Coordinator at Al-Anon Family Group Headquarters, an organization that serves the families and children of alcoholics throughout the world.

Dana E. Friedman began her career in Washington, D.C., as a lobbyist for the Day Care Council of America and the Coalition for Children and Youth. Since 1980 she has focused on private sector support to working parents. She conducted a national study of corporate views on family issues for the Carnegie Corporation of New York. That research led to the development of a national clearinghouse on work and family issues at The Conference Board, a nonprofit business research organization, where Dr. Friedman currently serves as a Senior Research Associate. She serves as a consultant to numerous corporations, government agencies and nonprofit organizations and has published widely on the subject of employer-supported child care.

Eli Ginzberg is Hepburn Professor Emeritus of Economics and Special Lecturer in Business, and Health and Society at Columbia University. He is also Director of the Conservation of Human Resources and of the Revson Fellows Program on the Future of the City of New York, Columbia University. He is a Fellow of the American Academy of Arts and Sciences and a member of the Institute of Medicine of the National Academy of Sciences. He has written more than ninety books on human resources and health policy.

Jerome Kagan is Professor of Human Development in the Department of Psychology at Harvard University. He is a member of the American Academy of Arts and Sciences and has served on private and public committees concerned with research in human development.

Sheila B. Kamerman is Professor of Social Policy and Planning at Columbia University School of Social Work and Co-Director of the Cross-National Studies Research Program at the School. She has carried out extensive research on comparative social and family policies.

Pamela Laber is Research Director of the Economic Policy Council. She received her B.A. degree from Barnard College of Columbia University and is currently pursuing a master's degree from the School of Organization and Management at Yale University.

Anna-Greta Leijon is Sweden's Minister of Labor and has been a member of the Swedish Parliament since 1973.

Daniel Patrick Moynihan, Democrat of New York, is the senior U.S. Senator from that state. He was elected in 1976, and re-elected in 1982. Senator Moynihan was previously a member of the Cabinet or sub-cabinet of Presidents Kennedy, Johnson, Nixon, and Ford. He was the U.S. Ambassador to India from 1973 to 1975 and the U.S. Permanent Representative to the United Nations in 1975–76. In February 1976 he became President of the United Nations Security Council. Senator Moynihan is the author, coauthor, or editor of thirteen books, including *Beyond the Melting Pot* (with Nathan Glazer), a study of ethnic groups of New York City that won the Anisfield-Wolf Award in Race Relations in 1963. His latest work is *Family and Nation*, based on the Godkin Lectures given last year at Harvard University. Senator Moynihan is a member of the Senate Finance Committee, the Budget Committee, and the Committee on Environment and Public Works. He is a member of the official U.S. Senate observer group to the arms talks between the United States and the Soviet Union, and he is also a member of the Senate Democratic Policy Committee.

Winn Newman, former General Counsel of several major international labor unions, is an attorney in private practice specializing in employment discrimination and labor law litigation. He has successfully pursued numerous lawsuits involving such forefront issues as pregnancy-based discrimination, union access to employer equal employment opportunity data, and sex- and race-based wage discrimination, resulting in millions of dollars in monetary relief for the victims of discrimination. He has written and lectured extensively on topics related to employment discrimination and is the recipient of several national awards for his work in this area. He holds degrees from the University of Wisconsin.

Christine L. Owens is an attorney in private practice, specializing in civil rights litigation with an emphasis on sex-based wage discrimination litigation. Formerly she served as Special Assistant to the Vice Chairman of the Equal Employment Opportunity Commission and as Consultant to the United States Senate Special Committee on Aging. She has written and lectured extensively on various employment discrimination issues and has taught graduate-level courses in this area. She holds degrees from the College of William and Mary and the University of Virginia School of Law.

Dallas L. Salisbury is President of the Employee Benefit Research Institute (EBRI), a Washington, D.C.-based public policy research organization dedicated to increasing knowledge and understanding of employee benefits. Prior to joining EBRI, Mr. Salisbury served in senior employee benefits regulatory policy positions at the Pension Benefit Guaranty Corporation and the pension and welfare benefit programs, U.S. Department of Labor. Before entering the employee benefits field, Mr. Salisbury held public and private sector positions in Washington, D.C., and Washington State. He attended the University of Washington and the Maxwell Graduate School in Syracuse, New York. He is a frequent author and speaker on employee benefit topics.

Albert Shanker has been President of the American Federation of Teachers, AFL-CIO, since 1974 and of its New York City local, the United Federation of Teachers, until 1985. He is president, as well, of the International Federation of Free Teachers' Unions, headquartered in Amsterdam, and is a vice president of the AFL-CIO, the first teacher to sit on its 35-person Executive Council. Most recently, Mr. Shanker was elected a member of the National Academy of Education.

Peter J. Sloane is the Jaffrey Professor of Political Economy and Head of Department at the University of Aberdeen, having previously held posts at the University of Aberdeen, the University of Nottingham, and Paisley College, where he was Professor of Economics and Management until 1984. He has also acted as Economic Adviser to the Department of Employment, and from 1979 until 1985 he was a Council Member of the U.K. Economic and Social Research Council. He is the author of several books and a number of papers on the economics of discrimination and has also published widely in other areas of labor economics and industrial relations, as well as on the economics of sports.

Hazel A. Witte is a consultant to the Employee Benefit Research Institute. She has also served in the Pension Welfare Benefit Program at the Department of Labor and as a consultant on employee benefits and health matters to both public and private institutions. Ms. Witte received her B.A. from Indiana University and J.D. from the State University of New York at Buffalo. She is a member of the District of Columbia Bar.

ABOUT THE EDITORS

Sylvia Ann Hewlett is Vice President for Economic Studies at the United Nations Association. She was born in Britain and educated at Cambridge, Harvard, and London Universities. She obtained her Ph.D. in economics in 1973. Between 1974 and 1981 she was Assistant Professor of Economics at Barnard College, Columbia University. Ms. Hewlett is the recipient of a Cambridge University Research Fellowship, a Lehrman Institute Fellowship, and numerous other awards. Her published works include *The Cruel Dilemmas of Development* (1980), *A Lesser Life: The Myth of Women's Liberation in America* (1986), and articles in *Foreign Affairs, Harpers,* the *New York Times, Family Circle,* and scholarly journals. She is a member of the Council on Foreign Relations.

Alice Stone Ilchman has been President of Sarah Lawrence College since 1981. Previously she served as Assistant Secretary of State for Educational and Cultural Affairs and later as Associate Director of the United States International Communication Agency in the administration of President Carter. From 1973 to 1978 she served as Dean of Wellesley College and Professor of Economics. She chaired the study group at the National Academy of Science/National Research Council, which produced in 1985 *Women's Work, Men's Work: Sex Segregation in the Work Place.* Dr. Ilchman is a member of the Smithsonian Council, the Markle Foundation Board of Directors, the Yonkers Emergency Financial Control Board, the NOW Legal Defense and Education Fund, and the Council on Foreign Relations. She has a B.A. from Mount Holyoke College and a Ph.D. from the London School of Economics.

John J. Sweeney is President of the 850,000-member Service Employees International Union, AFL-CIO, CLC, and a member of the Executive Council of the AFL-CIO. He is Chairman of the Council's Committee on Organization and Field Services and the Committee on Health Care and a member of the Evolution of Work and Its Implications Committee. He is a member of the Board of Governors of the American Red Cross and the Advisory Council of the Federal Mediation and Conciliation Services. In 1984 and 1985 he was a member of the U.S. delegation to the International Labor Organization in Geneva, Switzerland. He received his B.A. degree in economics from Iona College.